Street by Stree

G000293563

COLCHESTER
CLACTON-ON-SEA,
HARWICH

Brightlingsea, Dedham, Frinton-on-Sea, Halstead, Kelvedon, Manningtree, Tiptree, Walton-on-the-Naze, West Mersea, Wivenhoe

2nd edition June 2006
© Automobile Association Developments Limited 2006

Original edition printed August 2002

Ordnance Survey® This product includes map data licensed from Ordnance Survey® with the permission of the Controller of Her Majesty's Stationery Office. © Crown copyright 2006. All rights reserved. Licence number 399221.

Published by AA Publishing (a trading name of Automobile Association Developments Limited, whose registered office is Fanum House, Basing View, Basingstoke, Hampshire RG21 4EA. Registered number 1878835).

Mapping produced by the Cartography Department of The Automobile Association. (A02666)

A CIP Catalogue record for this book is available from the British Library.

Printed by Oriental Press in Dubai

The contents of this atlas are believed to be correct at the time of the latest revision. However, the publishers cannot be held responsible or liable for any loss or damage occasioned to any person acting or refraining from action as a result of any use or reliance on any material in this atlas, nor for any errors, omissions or changes in such material. This does not affect your statutory rights. The publishers would welcome information to correct any errors or omissions and to keep this atlas up to date. Please write to Publishing, The Automobile Association, Fanum House (FH12), Basing View, Basingstoke, Hampshire, RG21 4EA.

Ref: ML181z

Key to map pages	ii-iii
Key to map symbols	iv-1
Enlarged map pages	2-5
Main map pages	6-67
Index – towns & villages	68
Index – streets	68-74
Index – featured places	75
Acknowledgements	76

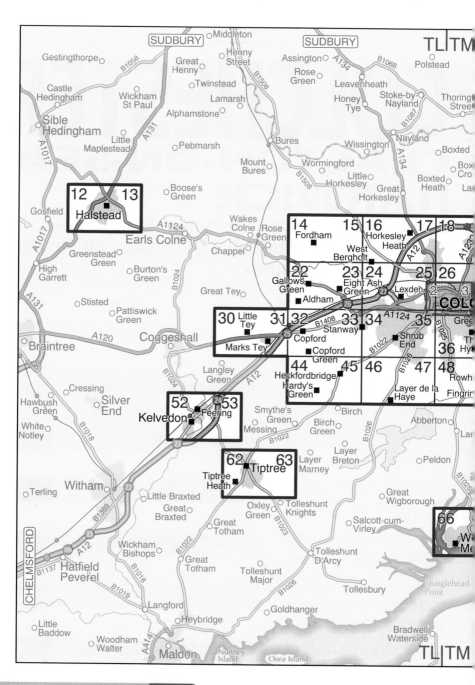

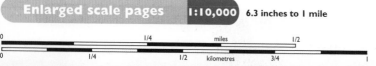

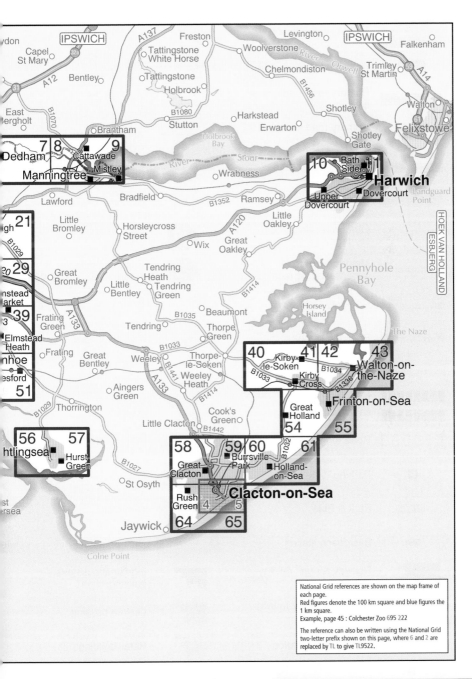

National Grid references are shown on the map frame of each page.
Red figures denote the 100 km square and blue figures the 1 km square.
Example, page 45 : Colchester Zoo 695 222

The reference can also be written using the National Grid two-letter prefix shown on this page, where 6 and 2 are replaced by TL to give TL9522.

4.2 inches to 1 mile

Scale of main map pages 1:15,000

| 0 | 1/4 | miles | 1/2 | | 3/4 | | 1 |
| 0 | 1/4 | 1/2 | kilometres 3/4 | 1 | | 1 1/4 | 1 1/2 |

iv

Junction 9	Motorway & junction	LC	Level crossing
Services	Motorway service area		Tramway
	Primary road single/dual carriageway		Ferry route
Services	Primary road service area		Airport runway
	A road single/dual carriageway		County, administrative boundary
	B road single/dual carriageway		Mounds
	Other road single/dual carriageway	17	Page continuation 1:15,000
	Minor/private road, access may be restricted	3	Page continuation to enlarged scale 1:10,000
	One-way street		River/canal, lake, pier
	Pedestrian area		Aqueduct, lock, weir
	Track or footpath	465 Winter Hill	Peak (with height in metres)
	Road under construction		Beach
	Road tunnel		Woodland
P	Parking		Park
P+	Park & Ride		Cemetery
	Bus/coach station		Built-up area
	Railway & main railway station		Industrial/business building
	Railway & minor railway station		Leisure building
	Underground station		Retail building
	Light railway & station		Other building
	Preserved private railway		

⊓⊓⊓⊓⊓⊓	City wall	♜	Castle
A&E	Hospital with 24-hour A&E department	🏛	Historic house or building
PO	Post Office	Wakehurst Place NT	National Trust property
📖	Public library	M	Museum or art gallery
ℹ	Tourist Information Centre	♞	Roman antiquity
ℹ	Seasonal Tourist Information Centre	⊥	Ancient site, battlefield or monument
⛽ ⛽	Petrol station, 24 hour Major suppliers only	🏭	Industrial interest
†	Church/chapel	❋	Garden
🚻	Public toilets	◉	Garden Centre Garden Centre Association Member
♿	Toilet with disabled facilities	🌷	Garden Centre Wyevale Garden Centre
PH	Public house AA recommended	🌳	Arboretum
🍽	Restaurant AA inspected	🛒	Farm or animal centre
Madeira Hotel	Hotel AA inspected	🦌	Zoological or wildlife collection
🎭	Theatre or performing arts centre	🦅	Bird collection
🎥	Cinema	🐋	Nature reserve
⚑	Golf course	🐟	Aquarium
▲	Camping AA inspected	V	Visitor or heritage centre
🚐	Caravan site AA inspected	♔	Country park
▲🚐	Camping & caravan site AA inspected	⌒	Cave
🎢	Theme park	🌾	Windmill
⛪	Abbey, cathedral or priory	🛢	Distillery, brewery or vineyard

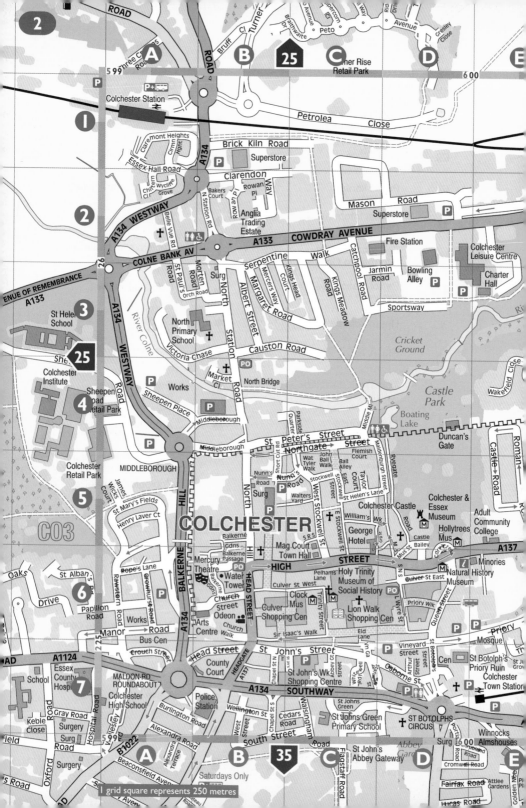

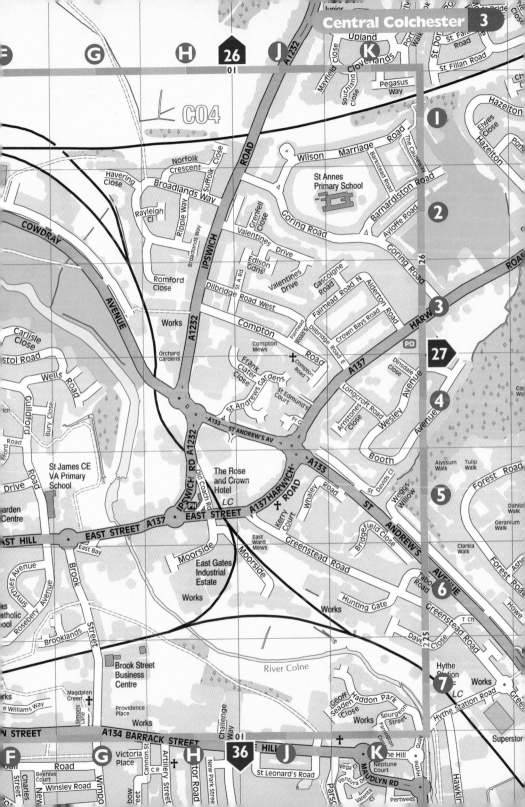

CO15

F
G
H
59
J
K

Vermont cl
Southcliff P.
HOLLA
Windsor School
Avenue

Clacton Leisure Centre

Clacton High School Performing Arts College

Boley Drive
Lyon Close
Reckitts
First Avenue
Second Av
Third Av
Fourth Av

Marine Parade East

I

Walton Road
Avondale Rd
College Rd
HOLLAND ROAD
Victoria Road
Albany Gardens
Lancaster Gardens East
Connaught Gardens East
Connaught Gardens West

Vista Road
sdale Road
Road
Road
Skelmersdale Rd
Albert Gardens
Lancaster Gardens West
Russell Road
Victoria Road
Gardens East
Marine Parade East

2

B1032
St Alban's Road
St Paul's Road
Ambleside Court

3

15

Thoroughgood Road
Vista Road
Church Road
Marine Parade East

Holland Road
Harold Road
Church Crs
Colchester Institute

4

CLACTON-ON-SEA

Esplanade Hotel

5

6

7

214

F
18
G
H
J
K
19

F
G
H
J
K

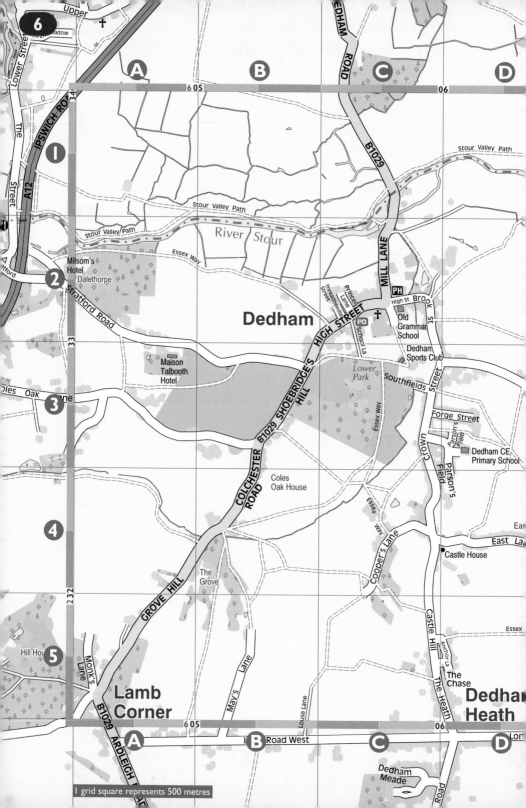

White Horse Road

B1070

MANN

Orvis Lane

Cordwinders

Dazeley

E

Fenbridge Lane

Flatford Road

F

G

Flatford Rd

Clapper Farm

H

07

08

34

Orvis Farm

I

Bridge

Stour Valley Path

Flatford Mill

Stour Valley

2

St Edmund Way

Flatford Bridge Cottage (NT)

33

Suffolk County

Essex County

3

Road

St Edmund Way

s

8

Way

Lower Barn Farm

Jupes Hill

4

232

Stour House

5

Essex Way

East Lane

Jupes

Hill

Mill

Hill

Long Road East

Hill Farm

Essex Way

Dedham

Road

E †

F

G

H

07

08

Bargat

WIGNALL ST

School La
Church Lane
Brantham Glebe
Rectory La

Elm Close
Cedar Cl
Drive
Sycamore
Way
Pine Cl
Grove Rd
Ash Gnd
Rise
nds
Brooklands
Prim Sch
Pattern Bush
Cl
Merriam
Cl

E
F
G
H
Newmill Lane

Court

Chase

Brantham Hall

I

awade

Works

2

34

33

Seafield Bay

3

4

232

Mistley Towers

Stour-Sailing Club
Quay St
B1352 THE WALLS
New Rd
The La
The Gn
HIGH STREET
Mistley
Anchor End
Anchor Lane
Portright
HIGH ST
Kiln La
Malthouse Rd
Erskine Rd
ROAD
Church Lane
PO
PH
Works
Mistley Station
Beckford Rd
California Rd
HARWICH
Stourview
Mistley Norman CE Prim Sch
Remercie Rd
Seafield Av
Stourview Cl
York St
Oxford Road
Norman Rd
Manifest Theatre
Barnfield
Essex Way
School Lane
Chpl Ct
HC
Swan Ct
Rigby

5

E
F
G
H
ROAD
B1352

Shrubland Road

Furze Hill

Middlefield Rd
Westmorland Close

NEW MISTLEY

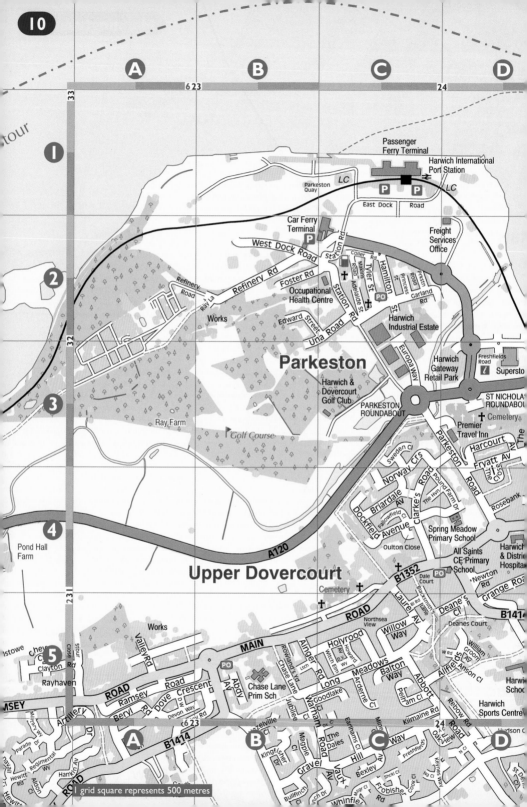

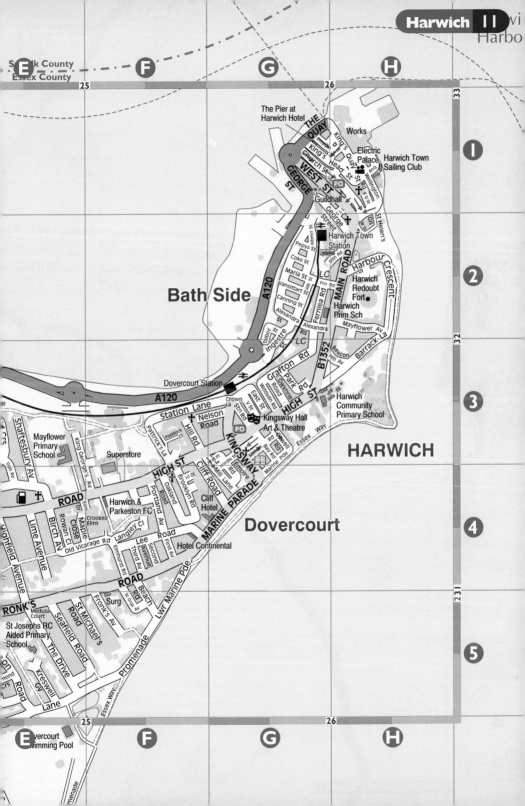

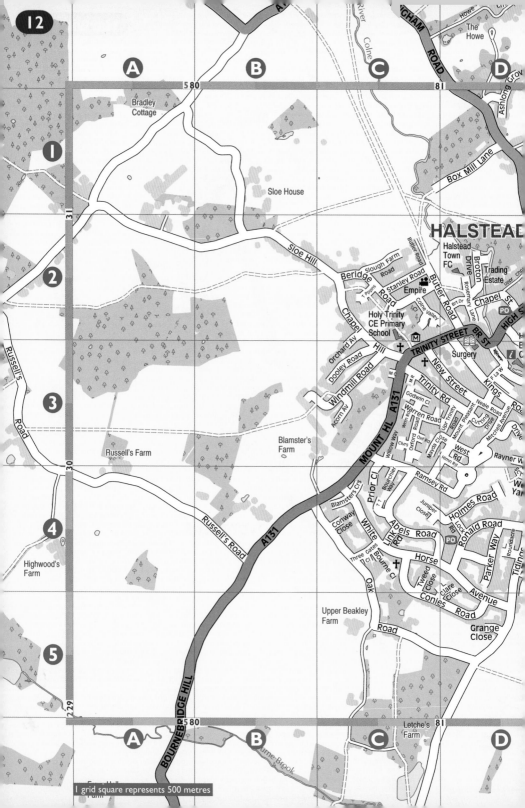

12

5 80

81

1

Bradley
Cottage

31

Sloe House

HALSTEAD

Halstead
Town
FC

Box Mill Lane

Ashling Grov

2

Sloe Hill

Slough Farm
Road

Beridge
Road

Stanley Road

Empire

Butler Road

Broton
Drive

Trading
Estate

Brt.Dr.

Rosemary Lane

Chapel
St

T Pgdns

Chapel Hill

Holy Trinity
CE Primary
School

Colne Valley

Upper Chap

PO

Russell's Road

Orchard Av

Dooley Road

Windmill Road

TRINITY STREET

Surgery

New Street

Kings

BR ST

HIGH S

3

30

Russell's Farm

Blamster's
Farm

Acorn Av

Mount Pleasant

Godwin Cl

Warren Road

MOUNT HL

A131

Willow Way

Butcher
Way

Oxf Rd

Clvrs

Trinity Rd

Upr Trinity

Neale Road

Curfong
Drive

Mitchell Avenue

West
Rd

Mayda Cl

Hlmn Rd

Rayner W

We
Ya

4

Highwood's
Farm

Blamsters Crs

Conway
Close

Prior Cl

White
Link
Rd

Bourne Cl

Three Gates

Oak

Ramsey Rd

Abels Road

Juniper
Close

LOCK

PO

Holmes Road

Ronald Road

Horse

Parker Way

Roundacre

Tidings

5

2 29

Upper Beakley
Farm

Road

Tweed
Close

Clare
Close

Conies
Road

Avenue

Grange
Close

5 80

81

BOURNEBRIDGE HILL

A131

Russell's Road

Burne Brook

Letche's
Farm

1 grid square represents 500 metres

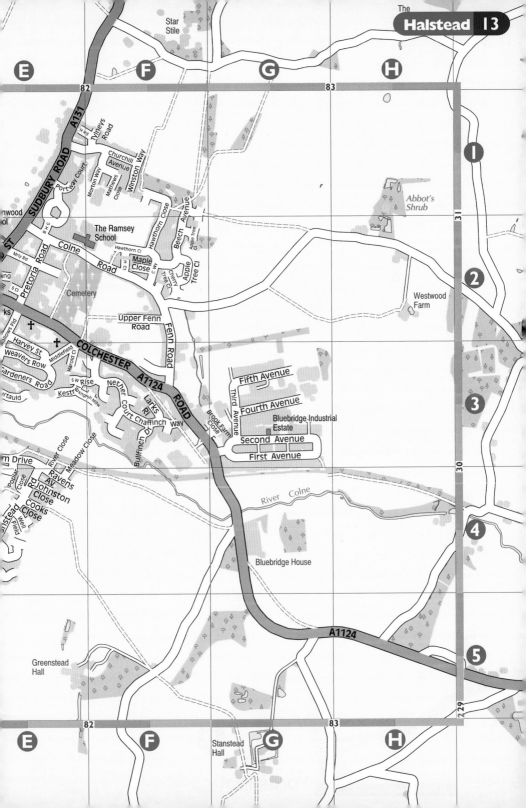

E   F   G   H

82   83

Star Stile

A131

H Rd

Tytleys Road

Portway Court

Churchill Avenue

Morton Way

Mathews Close

Winston Way

SUDBURY ROAD

BH G

Mrly Rd

S Cl

The Ramsey School

Coine Road

Pretoria Road

Hawthorn Cl

H Cl

Hawthorn Close

Beech Avenue

Apple Tree Cl

Maple Close

C W

Cherry Tree Cl

Apple Cl

Cemetery

Upper Fenn Road

Fenn Road

Hallows Fld

Harvey St

Weavers Row

Gardeners Road

Middlefield

Harold Cl

S W Rise

Kestr

Hingish Mow

Courtauld

COLCHESTER A1124 ROAD

Nether Court

Chaffinch Way

Larks Ri

Bullfinch Close

Meadow Close

River Close

m Drive

Poplar Close

Ravens AV

Johnston Close

Cooks Close

instead Close

Nell Field

Fifth Avenue

Fourth Avenue

Third Avenue

Brook Farm Close

Bluebridge Industrial Estate

Second Avenue

First Avenue

Abbot's Shrub

Westwood Farm

River Colne

Bluebridge House

A1124

Greenstead Hall

Stanstead Hall

31

2

30

2 29

I   2   3   4   5

E   F   G   H

82   83

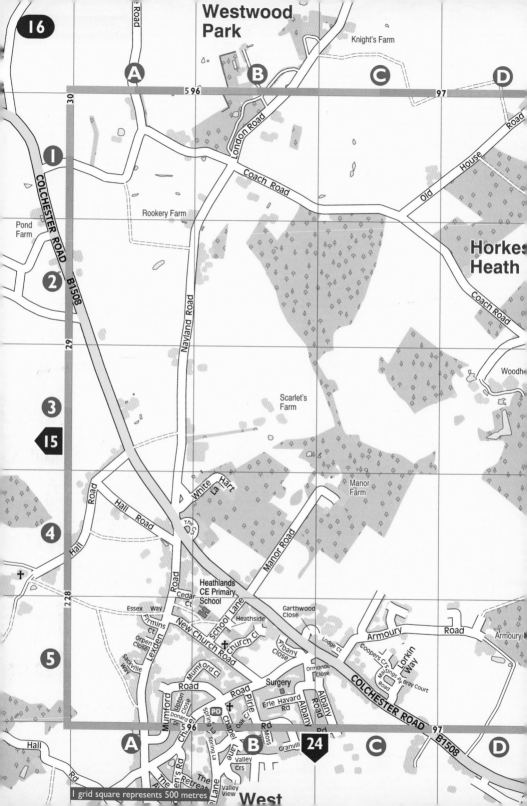

20

Ardleigh Heath

A B C D

6 04 05

I

Wick Lane

Fountain Farm

Fen Lane

EDHAM ROAD

THE S.

Moorhouse Green

Surgery

Ardleigh St Marys CE Primary School

Works

Mary Warner Road

Gernon Rd

Aveline

Rd

Blue

Dead Lane

2

29

Lodge Lane

Guide Post Farm

A137

Green Lane

Green Lane

Le

3

Lodge Lane

Lodge Farm

COLCHESTER ROAD

Martells Industrial Estate

19

Hill Farm

Redbury Farm

Martells Hall

4

Ardleigh Reservoir

Clover Way

Martells Industrial Estate

Slough Lane

2 28

5

Moze Hall

Hull Farm

Slough Lane

A B 28 C D

6 04 05

Crockleford Hall

A120

Springvalley

Jubile

Slough Farm

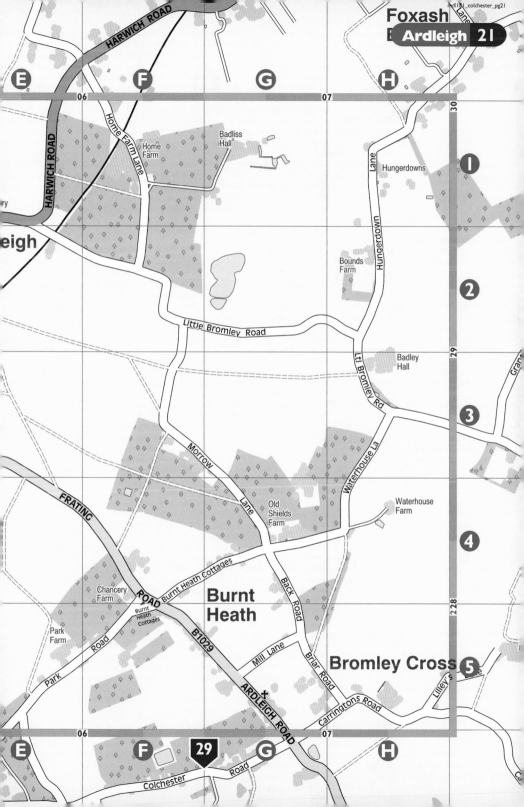

HARWICH ROAD

E   F   G   H

06   07   30

Home Farm Lane

Home Farm

Badliss Hall

HARWICH ROAD

Hungerdowns

Hungerdown Lane

I

eigh

Bounds Farm

2

29

Little Bromley Road

Ltl Bromley Rd

Badley Hall

Gran

3

Morrow Lane

Waterhouse La

FRATING

Old Shields Farm

Waterhouse Farm

4

228

Chancery Farm

Burnt Heath Cottages

Burnt Heath

Back Road

Park Farm

ROAD

Burnt Heath Cottages

Mill Lane

Briar Road

Bromley Cross

Lilley's Lane

5

Park Road

B1029

ARDLEIGH ROAD

Carringtons Road

E   F   **29**   G   H

06   07

Colchester   Road

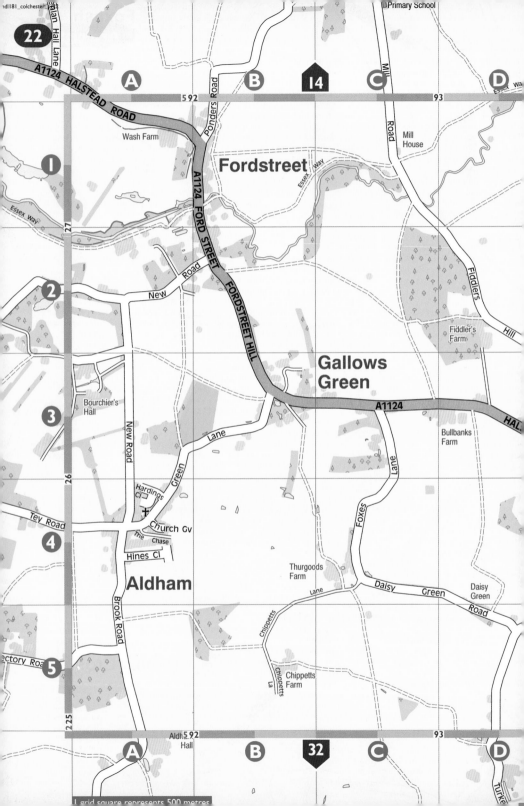

E F **I5** G H

94 95

I

River Colne

Great Porter's Farm

Cook's Hall

Cook's Hall Rd

Cook's Mill

Essex Way

Newbridge

27

2

Argents Lane

Chitts Hill

School Heath Road

White House Farm

Fordham Heath

Brick St

The Bridleway

3

26

24

Woodland Chase

Lane

Searle Way

Spring Lane

Heathfields

The Rise Walk

Chitts Hills

ROAD

†

Eight Ash Green

Iron Latch Lane

4

Blind Lane

PO

Holmw House Schoo

Abbots Lane

HALSTEAD RD-A1124

Halstead Rd

Halstead Road

5

Holiday Inn

Dale Cl

Lucy Lane N

Cowslip Ct

Cornflower Cl

Cl

Tudor Rose Ct

Sweet Briar Rd

Damask Cl

Musk Close

Road

A12

Provence

Lucy Lane South

Rugosa

Pede

Rambler Cl

25

Albertine Wk

Coralin

Tollgate

ESSEX

95

Sedge Cl

Spring

Daynprd

Ewan Cl

Lucy Cl

†

Millers Cl

Montbre

E F **33** G H

94 J26 95

MANRY WY-A1124

Beac End

24

A **B** **16** **C** **D**

Church Road
Church Cl
Orpen Close
Sackville Way
Lexden Ct
Mumford Cl
Albany Close
Lodge Ct
Armoury Road
Armoury

Surgery
Coopers Ct's
Maltings
2x Bray Court
Lorkin Way

Mumford Road
Chapel Road
Erie Havard Rd
Ormonde Close
COLCHESTER ROAD
B1508

PO
Spring La
Oak La
Moss
Rd
Granville Cl
97

I
Hall
Rd
The AV
Queen's Rd
The Retreat
Whitehouse La
Chapel Lane
Valley Crs
Valley View
West Bergholt

27
Newbridge
Bourne Road

2
Bourne Barn Farm
St Botolph's Brook

3
Chitts Hill

23

26

4
Cook's
Lane
Chitts Hills LC
A12
West
Bakers Lane
Lex
Go

J27

Latch Lane
Holmwood House School
Colchester Camping Caravan Park
A12
Spring
Le

5
Halstead Road
Lexden Squash Club
Chitts Hill
Firstore Drive
Beaver Close
Cook's Lane
Lexden Springs Special School
Lexden Ms
CYMBELINE WAY (COLCHESTER BY-PASS)
Spring La
Spring Lane
Tapwood

Tudor Rose
Musk Close
Rambler Close
Peace Road
King Coel
Mellor Cha
Halstead Road
Back
Marlowe Way

Sweet Briar Rd
Damask Road
Peace
25
Juniper
Fr Cl
Nelson Rd
Byron Av
Lexden Gv
Colvin Cl
Marlowe Mt

PO
LONDON ROAD A1124
5 96
97

A Beacon **B** **34** **C** Chaucer Way **D**
Montbretia Cl
Lexden Primary School
Wordsworth Road
Thompson Av
Herrick

1 grid square represents 500 metres

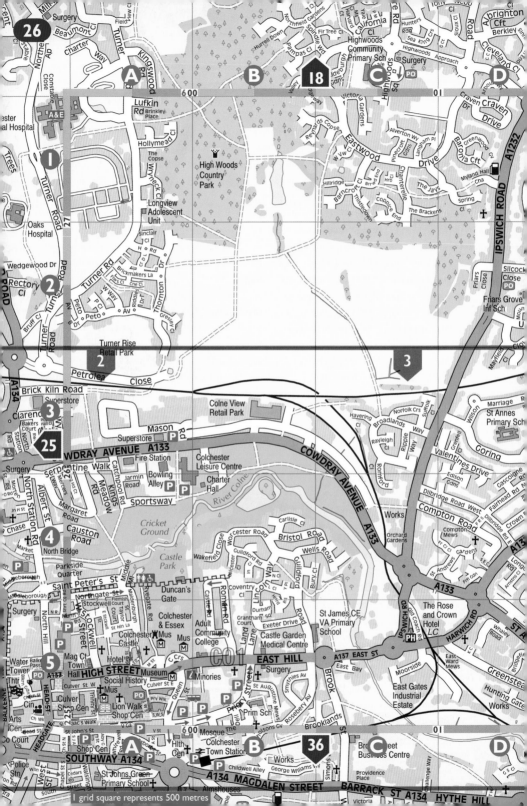

28

Moze
Hall

A 6 04 **B** Hull
Farm **20** **C** Slough Lane **D**

I

Crockleford
Hall

Springvalley Lane

A120

Jubilee
Lane

Slough
Farm

27

Salary Brook

2

Bromley Road

**Crockleford
Heath**

**Crockleford
Hill**

3

Green Lane

Chapel Lane

Wivenhoe Road

27

26

*Churn
Wood*

4

Peacock
Farm

Allen's
Farm

5

225

Slough Lane

Tye

A 6 04 **B** **38** **C** 05 **D**

I grid square represents 500 metres

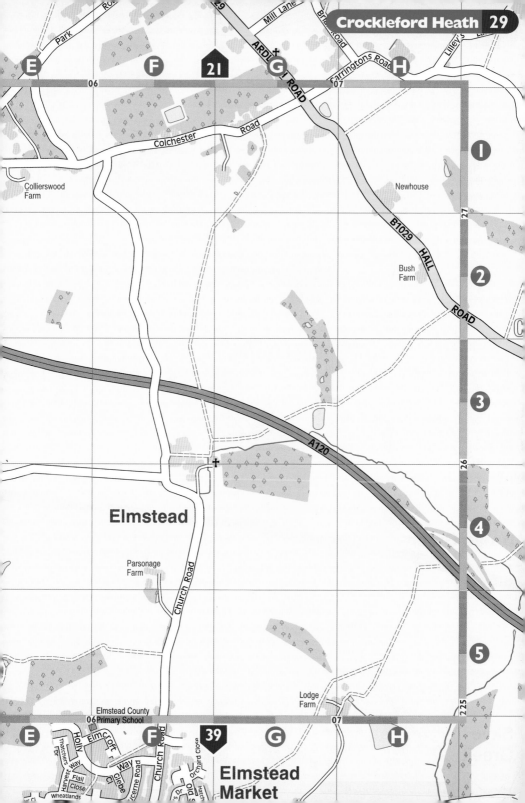

E F **21** G H

06 07

I

27

Park

Road

Mill Lane

Carringtons Road

Lilley's La

ARDL   G   ROAD

Colchester   Road

Newhouse

Collierswood
Farm

B1029   HALL

Bush
Farm

2

ROAD

C

3

A120

26

Elmstead

4

Parsonage
Farm

Church Road

5

225

Lodge
Farm

Elmstead County
06 Primary School

07

E F **39** G H

Holly
Elmcroft
Thatchers
Dr
Way
Harvest Way
Flail
Close
Wheatlands
Way
Glebe
Cl
Cerne Road
Church Road
Orchard Close
Hatch
Olds Rd

**Elmstead
Market**

Coggeshall Road

A 5 88 **B** **C** Essex Way 89 **D**

25

uckler's Farm

1

Farm

Dowsland
Green

Trumpingtons
Farm

Teybrook Farm

Essex Way

2

Roman Brook

24

Essex Way

East Gores Road **East Gores**

3

Upper Hall
Farm

Little
+ Tey

ouchin's Farm

Essex Way

Salmon's Lane

Church Lane

Great

4

Broad Green

Bracks Lane

COGGESHALL ROAD

Elm Farm

A120

223

Elm Lane

5

Lane

Mill Lane

5 88 89

**Skye
Green**

A **B** **C** **D**

Mill Lane

Hornigals

I grid square represents 500 metres

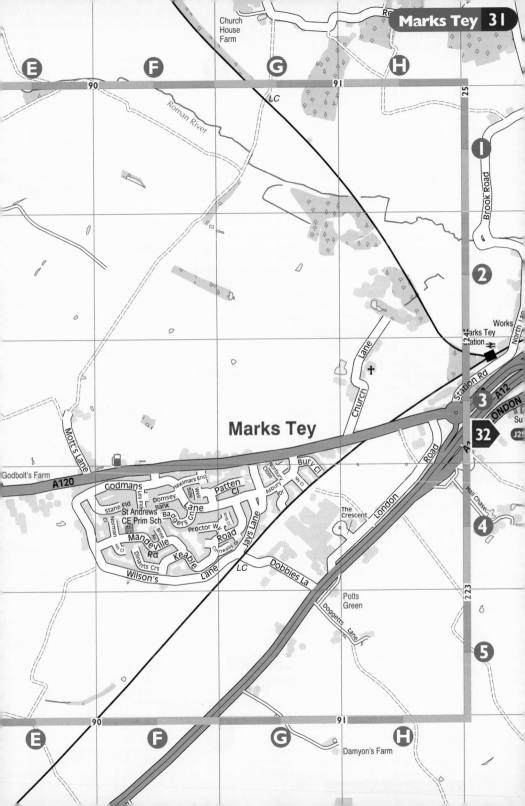

Church House Farm

Re

LC

E F G H

90 91 25

Roman River

I

Brook Rd

2

Works

Marks Tey Station

North La

Church Lane

3

Station Rd

A12

ONDON

32

J25

Su

Marks Tey

Mott's Lane

Godbolt's Farm

A120

Godmans

Stane Fld

Ley Flds

Domsey Bank

Hawlmark End

Patten Cl

Well Side

Norbury Close

Bury Cl

Asbury Dr

Wy Cl

St Andrews CE Prim Sch

Baggers Grn

Lane

Proctor W

Road

Norman

Mandeville Rd

Hn Cl

Dinants Crs

Keable Lane

Cornwallis Dr

Jays Lane

LC

Wilson's

Dobbies La

The Crescent

London Road

Hall Chase

4

Potts Green

Doggetts Lane

223

5

E F G H

90 91

Damyon's Farm

E F **23** G H

I

2

3 **34**

4

5

E F **45** G H

Map labels:

Holiday Inn
Abbo...
Dale Cl
LUCY Lane N
Cowslip
Cornflower
Centaur
Sweet Briar Rd
Musk Close
Rambler Cl
Close
Roa...
Rugosa Cl
Jubilee Cl
Coralli... Wk
Albertine Wk
Peace
LUCY Lane south
Damask Road
Spring Cl
Ewan Cl
Ewan Wy
Miles
LUCY Cl
Wd En Beacon Way
Barn Flds
Dawnford Cl
Millers Cl
Millers Lane
New...
Winstree Rd
Montt...
Bea End
Tollgate Road
Tollgate East
Surgery
Chapel Road
Stanway Primary School
The Heat... Scho... Brough... Glades...
Wd En
Marram
Mr O Cl
Darnel Cl
Spode Cl
J26
ESSEX YEOMANRY WY – A1124
Tollg 95
112
D–A1124
Tollgate West
Tollgate West
Tollgate Road
CO3
Stanway
Nursery Cl
Stanway School
Wyvern Farm
LONDON RD B1408
Villa
Winstree Rd
Wyevale Garden Centre
LONDON ROAD B1408
St Marys Lower School
Stanway Swimming Centre
Juniper Road
Harvey Crs
Harvey Wy
Gorse Wy
Gorse Rd
Holly
Rowan Cl
Church La
Church Lane
Robin
Crescent
Crane Av
Crnc Av
LWk
Sandmartin
Right Pl
Cygnet Wk
Crs
Swift Av
Wren Cl
Warren Lane
Bailey
Dale
Blackberry
Rose Av
Pearmain Way
Egremont
Grieves...
Tydeman Close
Rowan Road
Lambourne Cl
PO
Dyer's
Bellhouse Farm
Sta Gre
Roman River
Warren Lane
Upper Hill Farm
MALDON
94
95
94
95
223
25...

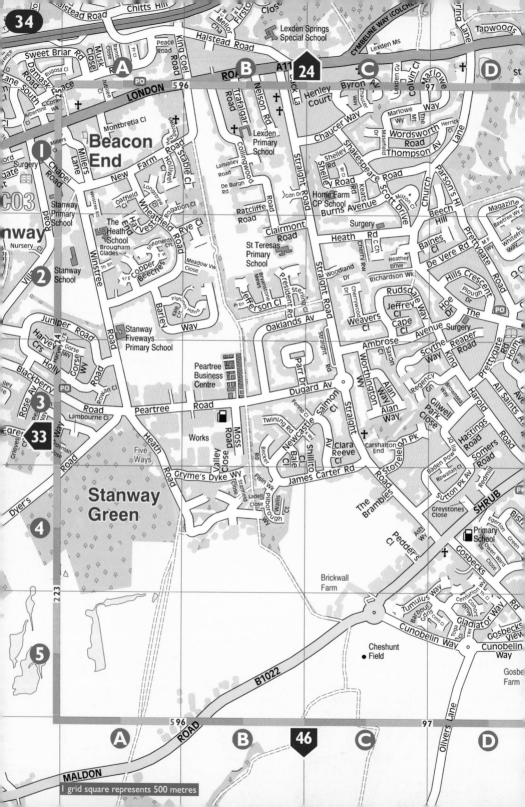

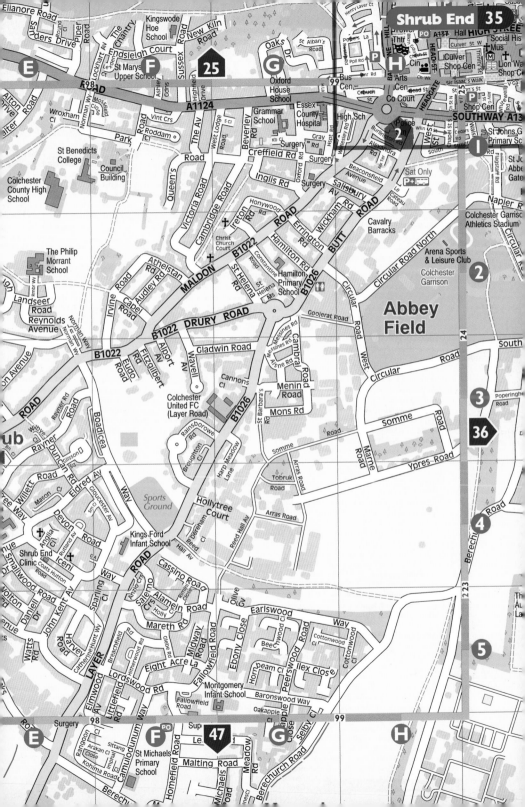

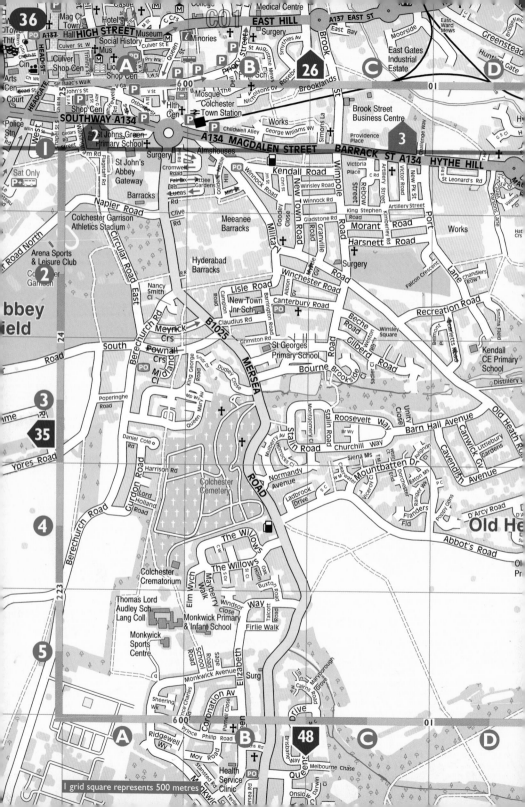

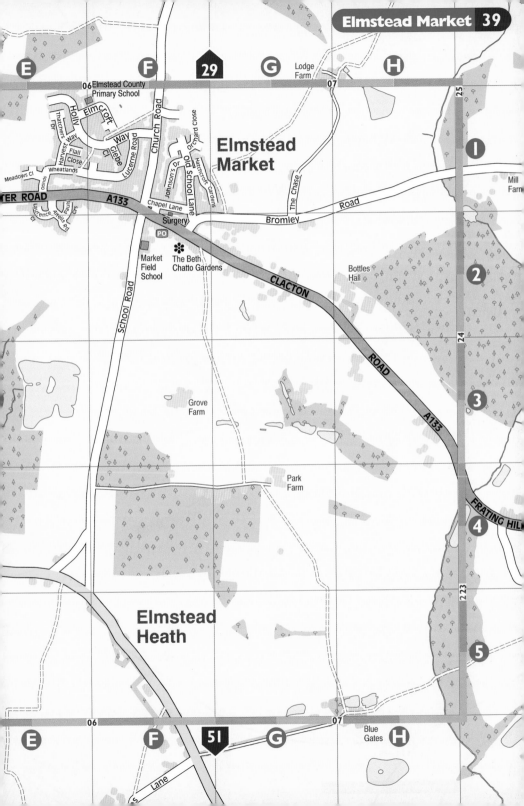

E F 29 G Lodge Farm H

06 Elmstead County Primary School

Elmcroft

Holly

Thatchers Dr

Harters Way

Flail Close

Glebe

Wheatlands

Meadows Cl

Lucerne Road

Church Road

Old School Lane

Johnson's Dr

Orchard Close

Hatchcroft Gardens

Elmstead Market

TER ROAD

A133

Laurence Cl

Tyrrells Rd

Pains Cl

Chapel Lane

Surgery

PO

Market Field School

The Beth Chatto Gardens

School Road

Bromley

The Chase

Road

CLACTON

Bottles Hall

I

Mill Farm

2

24

ROAD

A133

3

Grove Farm

Park Farm

FRATING HILL

4

223

Elmstead Heath

5

06 E F 51 G 07 Blue Gates H

S Lane

40

Walton Road

New Hall

Ⓐ Ⓑ Kentshill Farm 20 Ⓒ Ⓓ

619 23

Walton Road

I

Farm Lane

Byng rs

2

Sneating Hall

FRINTON 22

White Ldg Crs

Damant's Farm

ROAD

B1033

SNEATING HALL LANE

B1054

King's Farm

3

Thorpe Cross

4

B1033

THORPE

5

Thorpe Park

221

Pork Lane

LC Birch Hoe Farm

619 Ⓐ Ⓑ 20 Ⓒ Ⓓ

I grid square represents 500 metres

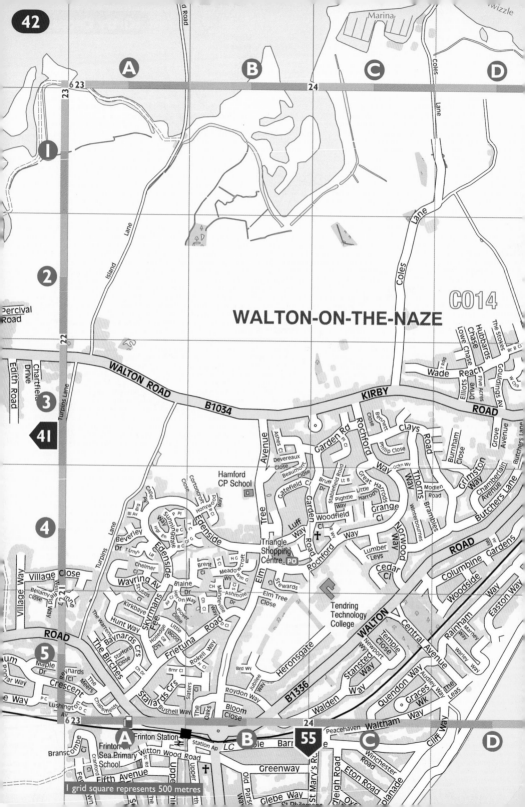

E F G H

27 23

I

Second Avenue
First Avenue
Third Av
Road
26
Naze Park
Hamford Cl
ALDPH
PO Spendells Cl
Florence Rd
Greville Cl
Beatrice Road
Cliff Parade
Percival Rd
High Lane
Ter Cl
Green Lane
M The Frinton &
Walton Heritage Museum

2

Walton &
Frinton
Yacht Club

Hall Lane
East Terrace

Frinton & Walton
Swimming Pool
Walton
Primary
Sch
P
Standley
Rd
Eagle
PRINCE'S ESP
Saville Street
N St
Cl
22

Surg
PO
i

3

Mill Lane

Marina Mews
Churchfield
Rd
West St
Martello
Portobello
Old Pier St
Sfn St
HIGH STREET
Alf Ter
New Pier St
VICTORIA Rd
Station Street
Church
street
ARA
The
Parade
Pier Approach
Walton Pier

4

221

5

E F G H
26 27

A **B** **Copford Green** **32** **C** **D**

School Road

St Michael's Cha

Orchard Cl

Church Road

5 92

93

I

22

Little Birch Holt Farm

Rectory Road

Fountain Lane

2

Bockingham Hall Farm

Easthorpe Road

Easthorpe

Churchwell Avenue

3

21

Whitehouse Farm

Well Lane

4

Hellen's

Hardy's Green

Beckin Hall

nterflood's m

Shemmings Farm

5

Ca d's Farm

220

5 92

93

A Blind Lane **B** **C** **D**

Brake

1 grid square represents 500 metres

Roman River

E

F

33

G

H

94

95

Warren Lane

MALDON

I

22

Upper Hill Farm

Fountain Lane

Colchester Zoo

2

Heckfordbridge

Lukes Farm

3

Birch Business Centre

ROAD

46

21

MALDON

Orpen's Hill

Leas Lane

4

B1022

Birch Hall

Conduit Farm

5

220

Lower Road

94

95

E

B1022

Birch

F

Sch Hill

†

G

H

Birch Primary School

Caper

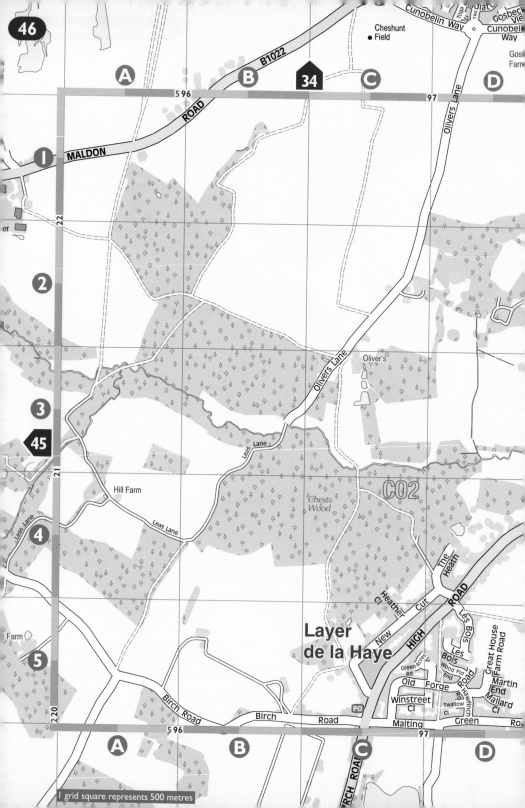

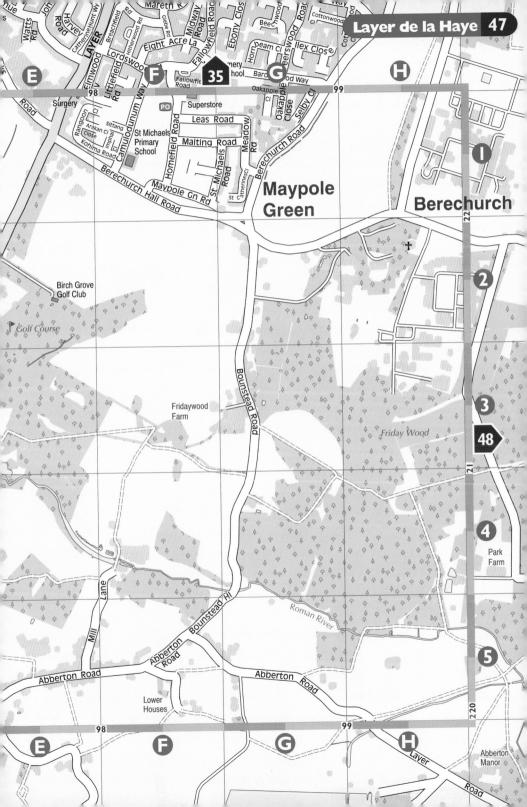

Watts Rd

Harvey Road

Elmwood

LAYER

Lordswood

Littlefield Rd

Mareth Rd

Midway Road

Fallowfield Road

Eight Acre La

Ebony Clos

Hornbeam Cl

Beech

Deerswood Road

Ilex Close

Cottonwood Cl

Cottonwood Way

E

F

35

G

H

I

98

99

22

Surgery

Camulodunum Way

Rangoon

Arakan Cl

Sittang

Kohima Road

PO

Homefield Road

St Michaels Primary School

Superstore

Leas Road

Malting Road

Meadow Rd

Berechurch Road

Oakapple Close

Selby Cl

Maypole Gn Rd

St Michaels Road

St Catherine's

Berechurch Hall Road

Maypole Green

Berechurch

2

Birch Grove Golf Club

Golf Course

Bounstead Road

Fridaywood Farm

Friday Wood

†

3

48

4

Park Farm

21

Mill Lane

Bounstead Hl

Abberton Road

Roman River

5

Abberton Road

Abberton Road

Lower Houses

220

E

F

98

G

99

H

Layer Road

Abberton Manor

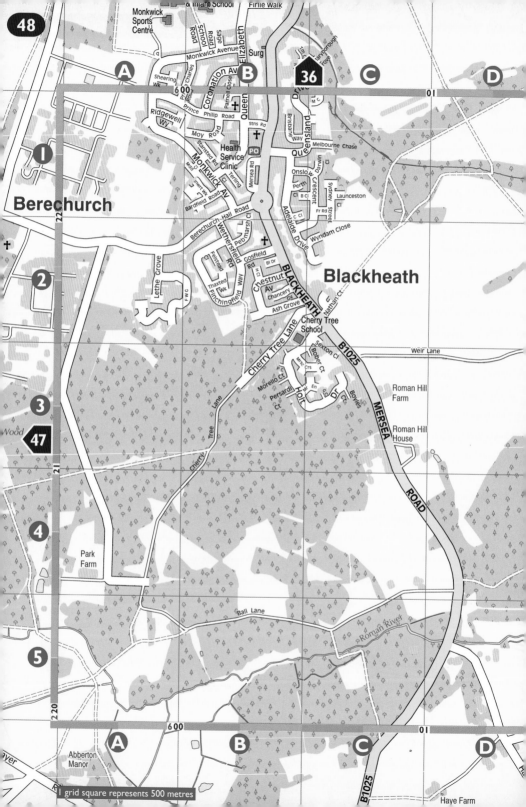

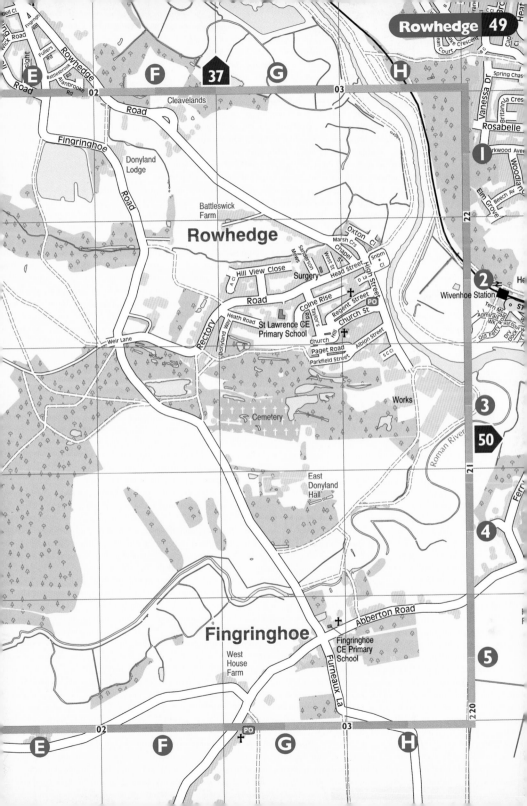

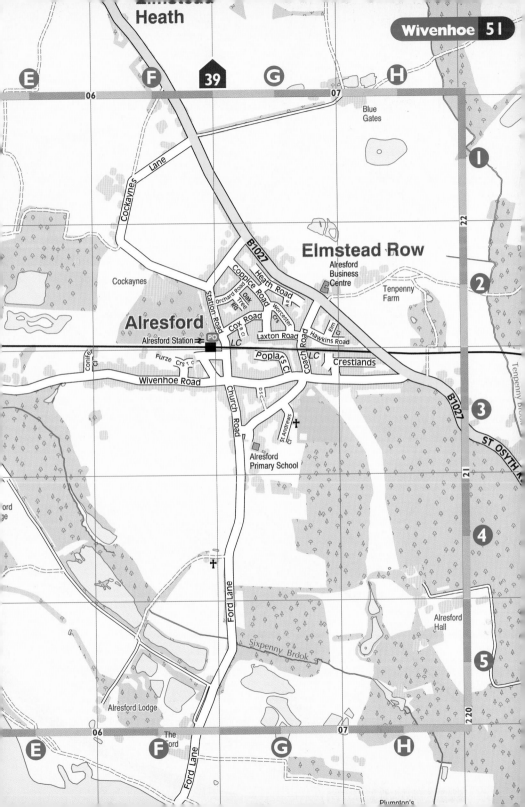

Elmstead
Heath

E F **39** G H

Blue
Gates

Cockaynes Lane

I

22

B1027

Elmstead Row

Alresford
Business
Centre

Tenpenny
Farm

2

Cockaynes

Coppice Road

Heath Road

Orchard Road

Tree Rd

Oak

Worcester Cres

Station Road

Alresford

Alresford Station

PO

COX Road

Laxton Road

Elm

Hawkins Road

Coach Road

LC

LC

Crestlands

Poplars Cl

Furze Crs

Conifer Cl

Wivenhoe Road

Crestlands

Tenpenny Brook

B1027

3

ST OSYTH A

21

Church Road

St Andrews

Alresford
Primary School

4

Alresford
Hall

Ford Lane

Sixpenny Brook

5

2 20

Alresford Lodge

E F G H

The Ford

Ford Lane

06 07

06 07

Plumpton's

A **B** **C** **D**

5 85 86

20

1

Monk's Farm

Pantlings Lane

White Barn

Frame Farm

Coggesh Hall

River Black

Coggeshall

2

Observer Way

B1024

River Blackwater

Rye

Sherwood W

Mr Cl

Hunt Close

Driffield Close

19

3

Park Farm

Kelvedon Station

Industrial Estate

Doucecroft Sch

PO

Dowches Drive

T Gdns

B Pl

Orchard

D Gdn

Mtnd Cl

Kingsley Wy

Feering

FEERING HILL

Works

Worlds

Barnfield

End

Bittern Close

Avocet

Swan Street

Tern Close

Heron Rd

Lane

4

Road

Felix Place

LC

Cemetery

Glebe Road

Thorne Road

New Road

Church Road

Rolley La

Firs Cl

St Mary's Road

HIGH STREET

B1024

Canonium Mews

St Mary's Road

The Chase

Docwra Road

Kelvedon St Marys CE Cont Sch

Ct Rd

Gd Gr

Lpwn

Ward Cl

Curlew Close

Teal Way

Riverside Way

Dunlin Court

KELVEDO

5

Clark's Farm

Church Street

Church Hall

The Cloisters

Easterford Road

Brockwell Lane

Maldon

LONDON ROAD

B1024

Ewell

Hall

Chase

Hall

Ewell Hall

18

Cranes

Crabb's

Lane

5 85 86

A **B** **C** **D**

E
F
G
H

Travelodge

Long Acres

Hanover
Bridge
The Street
New Lane
J24

88
89

I

20

B1024

Cemetery

LONDON RD

B1024

rs Mead
l Rd

Gore Pit

A12

Prested
Hall
†

Domsey Brook

2

INWORTH ROAD

Threshelfords
Business
Park

3

B1023

19

Threshelfords
Farm

Yewtree Farm

Park Farm

4

Kelvedon

Parsonage
Farm

Ne

B1023

5

218

Messing Par

Inworth
88
89

E
F
G
H

†

ON-ON-SEA

Frinton Station

Frinton on Sea Primary School

Fifth Avenue

Upr Second Av

Holmbrook Way

Upper Third Av

Upper Fourth Avenue

The Close

Witton Wood Road

Old Parsonage Way

Greenway

Glebe Way

St Mary's Rd

Hadleigh Road

Winchester Road

Eton Road

Oxford Road

Cambridge Road

Esplanade

St Philomena School

The Crescent

Raglan Road

Frinton Summer Thtr

Ashlyn's Rd

Queen's Road

Harold Way

Harold Gvd

Harold Road

Old Way

Old Road

B1035 CONNAUGHT AVENUE

First Avenue

First Av

Second

Third

Fourth

Road

Avenue

Avenue

Holland

Esplanade

Surgery

Esplanade

The Greensward

Frinton Golf Club

n-Sea nis Club

Course

Holland Gap

Station Ap

LC

Pole Barn Lane

Peacehaven

Waltham Way

Cliff Way

PO

Baynards Crs

e Bitches

Stallards

Bushell Way

Frietuna

Heronsgate

College

Temple Close

ntral Avenue

Rain

Stansted Way

Newport Way

Quendon Way

Graces Wk

The Leas

Royce

Jubilee

Bloom Close

The Oaks

Brd Wy

Iden Way

Audrey Way

Frinton on

Witton Wood Road

Moverons

Moverons Lane

Wapping Lane

Moverons Lane

B1029

CHURCH ROAD

08

6 07

Samso
Corner

1

Samson's

Fordwich Rd
St Romney Close
St Andrews Place
Maltings

Deal Way
Sarre Way

CHURCH RD

The C
Comm
Schoo

2

18

BRIGHTLINGSEA

Manor House Way
Pertwee
Upper Park Rd

3

17

Marennes
Crescent
Pyefleet

Lodge Lane
Dean Street
Chestnut
Well Str

Park

Elm Dr
Ash Cl
Hazel
Walnut Way

Cedar Av
Planton Way
Willow Close
Birch Cl

Bright
J&I Sc

Beacon Cl
Lower Park Rd

Marsh Way
York
Wester

4

Colne
Medical Cen

5

Westmarsh
Point

Promenade
Western Prom
Way

Oyster

Brightlingse
Sailing Club

216

6 07

08

St Osyth
Stone Point

East Essex
Aviation Society

1 grid square represents 500 metres

E F G H

Morses

Lowermarsh
Farm

Campernell
Close

Folkards Lane

Barn Road

Dover Road

Red

W P
H PI

Regent Cl

Sandwich Road

Cinque Road

Kent Dover Rd

Port Road

Bellfield Av

Bellfield Close
Bellfield Close

Stoney Lane

Robinson Road

Lower
Farm

Brightlingsea
United FC

View Gdns

Regent

Stanley Av

Chapel Road

Granville Way

Freelands

Freelands

Bayard Av

George Av

Beaumont Avenue

H H C

Greenhurst Road

Edward Avenue

Springfields

Richard Road

Albert Rd

Whitegate Rd

Creekhurst Close

Queen St

Elizabeth Wy

John St

K Cl

Charles

Anne Cl

Hurst Close

Chapel Rd

Fair Close

PO

High Street

Tower Cut

Gr C

**Hurst
Green**

Mill

Street

Link Rd

Back Waterside Lane

Tower Street

Lime Street

Works

University
Yacht Club

Colne
Yacht Club

Brightlingsea Creek

E F G H

Cindery
Island

Brightlingsea Creek

Flag C

St Os

1
2
3
4
5

09 10 216 17 18

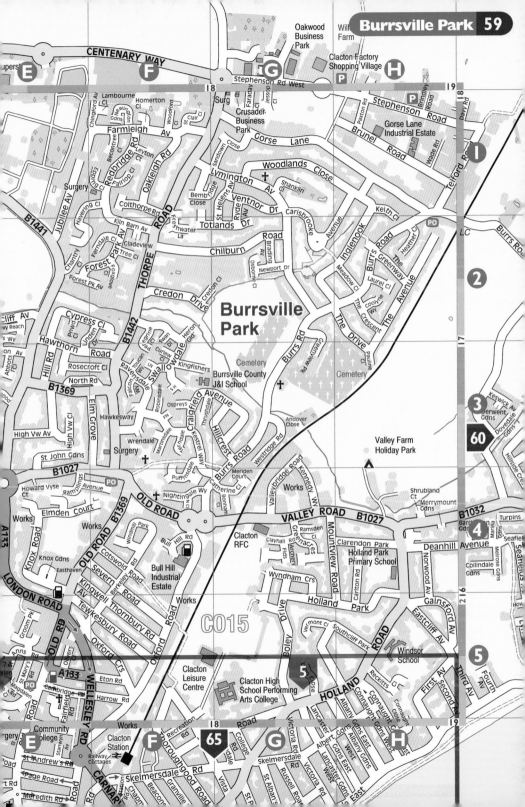

Holland Brook

LC

A B C D

619 18 20

Sladbury's Old House

Pond House

Brindley Road

P

henson Road

orse Lane dustrial Estate

Davy Rd

Road

1

Heather Cl

The

PO

LC

Burr's Road

Telford Road

Picker's Ditch

2

Avenue

Keswick Gdns

Derwent Gdns

Dovedale Gdns

Hillside Crescent

Windermere Rd

Slade Road

Brentwood Road

Chelmsford Road

Colchester Road

Ipswich Rd

Stratford Road

Nansen Road

Merrilees Crs

Norman Road

Fleetwood

Fd Cl

Pickers Way

Avenue

Broadmere Cl

Suffolk Cl

Elmfield

Grenfell

Norfolk

Oakwood Avenue

Avenue

Park Blvd

Briarwood

Av

Aylesbury Drive

Viking Wy

Saxon Wy

Surgery

3

y Farm ay Park

59

Surgery

FRINTON ROAD

Frinton Road Medical Cen

Surgery

Kent's Av

Hckls Av

Pembroke Gdns

Sussex Gdns

Holland Haven Prim Sch

Primrose

Hereford Road

Manchester Rd

Nottingham Rd

Kenilworth Rd

York Road

Ingarfield Rd

Edison Road

Brighton Road

Brimhill Cl

Surgery

4

Shrubland Ct

Merrymount Gdns

B1032

Barrington Gdns

Turpins Cl

Seafields Gdns

Collindale Gdns

Deanhill Avenue

Norwood Av

Melrose Gdns

Mersea Gdns

Turpins Av

Hillside Crs

Preston Road

Bedford Road

Kings Avenue

Salisbury Road

Dulwich Road

Queensway

Princes Rd

Madeira Road

Dulwich Rd

PO

Cliff Road

Canterbury Road

The Parade

Chase

Fernwood Av

Holland-on-Sea

Kings

5

Windsor School

Gainsford Av

Eastcliff Av

First Av

Second Av

Third Av

Fourth Av

Howard Rd

Seafields Rd

Hazlemere Rd

Lyndhurst Rd

Madeira

Kings Parade

A B C D

619 18 20

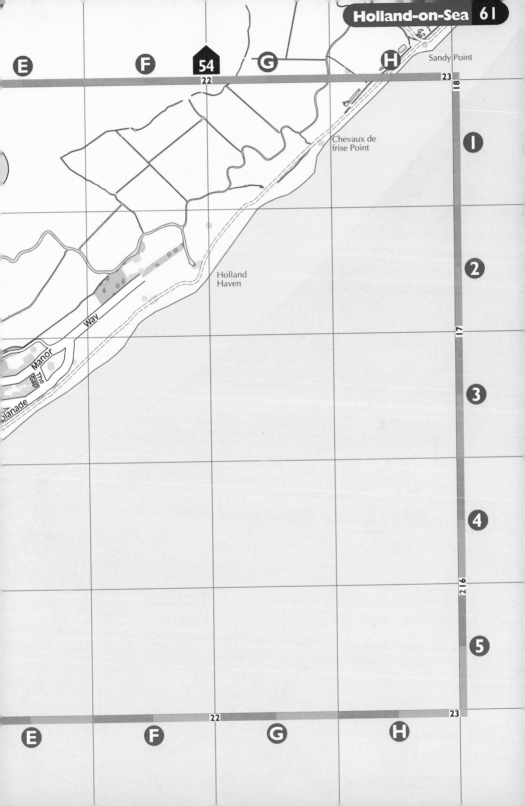

E

F

54

22

G

H
Sandy Point

23
18

Chevaux de
frise Point

1

Holland
Haven

2

17

3

Manor
The Gap
lanade
Way

4

216

5

22
23

E

F

G

H

A B C D

5 88 89

Hill Farm

1

17

KELVEDON
Oak Road
Rookery Lane
Road
Cedar A
Tower Business Park
Baynards Primary School
ROAD
Townsend Rd
Oak
W Wk
Elm Close
Chestnut
Walnut Tree Way
Maple Leaf
Pit Lane
Behz La

2

B1023
Vine
Lnsm Cl
Prlm La
Spores Road
Kingsway
Queensway
W Wk
Mill Close

TIPTREE
Grange Road
Harrington Close
Ranse Road
W Wk
Perry Rd
Blue Road
Pennsylvania Lane
MALDON ROAD
Holly Way
Rosemary Crs
Remy Cl

3

16
New Plantation

Brook Mdws
Anchor
B1022
Cirksm
Saffron Wy

4

Inworth Grange

Peakes Close
Francis Cl
Spring Rd
Stat
Surrey Lane
Birkin Close
Bull Lane

Tiptree Heath

Tiptree Heath Primary School
Hall Road

5

215
Priory Road
West End Road
Simpsons Lane
Tiptree

A B C D

5 88 stone Lane 89
Lane
Tiptree Hall

1 grid square represents 500 metres

Tiptree Priory

Wood

Haynes Green

Haynes Green Road

E F G H

B1022

90 91

 TER ROAD

Newbridge Road

I

Tiptree Sports Centre

Viners Farm

School fields

17

2

Milldene Primary School

Works

Lane

Heycroft Way

Grove Road

Wilkin Dr

Tawell

B Cl

Warren

Ling

Oller Wk

Brassingham Crescent

Grove Road

Newbridge Road

3

Anchor Press Social & Sports Club

Kersey

Wilkin Dr

Southgate Crescent

Luther

Tiffin Dr

Kittle Road

b W

Works

Grosvenor Close

Seldon Road

Elwin Road

Shelley

Wadley

Wadley Cl

Archer Crs

Winnin

Biddon Close

Churchill Road

16

PO

New Road

Keeble Close

Gager Dr

Winston Avenue

Birchwood Way

4

St Lukes Church Primary School

Bird Lane

Chapel Road

Birchwood Close

Morley Road

B1023

Tiptree Museum

Bainbridge Drive

Paternos Heath

Cherry Chase

FACTORY HILL

Layer Brook

5

te House

Tudwick Road

Brook Close

Strawberry La

D'ARCY ROAD

Knights Cl

PO

Brook Road

The Folly

215

90 91

E F G H

Hawthorn Road

Stockhouse Cl

Blackthorn Way

Tolleshunt Knights

Rouses Farm **1**

Bishops Park College

Rush Green

Bishops Park College

Rush Green Sports Centre

St Clares RC Prim Sch

Ravenscroft Prim Sch

58

Douglas Road

Coppins Road

Colbayns High School

Saxmundham Way

Tyler Av

Jaywick Lane

2

Elm Gv
Oak Av
Poplar
Av
Chestnut
Av
Woodland
Virginia Cl
Drakes Rd

Seymour Road
Frobisher
Drive
Somerset
Leicester
Cl
Spenser
Way

Frobi
Prim School **3**

Miller's Barn Rd
Chaucer Cl
Tudor Cl
Richmond Drive
Tyndale Drive

Alton Park Lane

Clacton Airfield

Cherry Tree Avenue

Crown Road
Queen's Road
King's Road
Arnold Road
Park Way
Coan Avenue
West Rd

The Leas Special School

Oakwood Infant School

Alton Junior School

Marlowe Road
Square East
Alleyne Way
Donne Drive
Union Way

Tudor
Green **4**
Boleyn Way
Crossways

Park

Community Care & Health Centre

PO

Golf Course

Clacton-on-Sea Golf Club

Brixham Cl

Portsmouth Road
Hastings Avenue
Deal Rd

Jaywick **5**

Jasmine Wy
Cornflower Way
Rosemary Way
New Glebe Way
Garden Road
Green Road

Meadow
Fern Way
Lake Wy
Christophers Wy
Willow Wk
Lavender Wk
Flowers Wy
Broadway

Horse Way

Tamarisk Way
Beach Way

PO

P

1 grid square represents 500 metres

A   B   C   D

CLACTON-ON-SEA

Clacton Leisure Centre

Clacton High School Performing Arts Col

HOLLAND

59

Works

Clacton Station

Railway Cottages

Community College

St Andrew's Rd

Page Road

Meredith Rd

Pier Avenue Cinema

Old Road

Surgery

Rosemary Rd West

Police Stn

Beatrice Rd

Clacton & District Hospital

Parade

Town Hall

Covered Market

PO

Chudleigh Hotel

Esplanade Hotel

Clacton Pier

Colchester Institute

St Alban's Rd

Marine Parade East

WELLESLEY RD

CARNARVON ROAD

HIGH STREET

A133

Skelmersdale Road

Thoroughgood Rd

Walton Road

Victoria Road

5

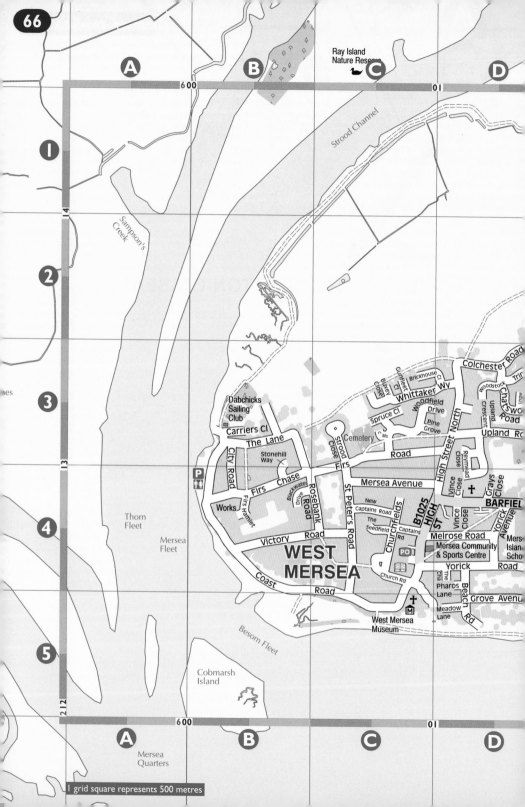

A 600 B Ray Island Nature Reserve C 01 D

I

14

Sampson's Creek

Strood Channel

2

3

13

Dabchicks Sailing Club

Carriers Cl

The Lane

Stonehill Way

Cemetery

City Road

Firs Chase

P

Works.

Firs Hamlet

Thorn Fleet

Mersea Fleet

4

Victory

Coast

WEST MERSEA

Road

Road

Firs

Strood Close

St. Peter's Road

Rosebank Road

Blackwater Drive

Gunfleet Cl

Buxey Close

Brickhouse Cl

Whittaker Wy

Woodfield Drive

Spruce Cl

Pine Grove

Woodstock Cl

Colchester Road

Upland Crescent

Chatsworth Road

Upland Rd

High Street North

Reymead Close

Vince Close

Grays Close

Road

Mersea Avenue

New Captains Road

The Seedfield

Captains Rd

Churchfields

B1025 HIGH ST

Vince Close

Vince Close

BARFIEL

Melrose Road

PO

Mersea Community & Sports Centre

M

Yorick Avenue

Mersea Island School

Church Rd

Yorick Road

The Pharos Lane

Meadow Lane

Beach Rd

Grove Avenue

West Mersea Museum

5

Besom Fleet

Cobmarsh Island

212

600 01

A Mersea Quarters B C D

1 grid square represents 500 metres

Mersea Island

Bower Hall

Haycocks

Bocking Hall

C05

East Mersea Road

Bower Hall Lane

Blue Row

Haycocks Lane

Chapmans Lane

Wellhouse Farm

Weathercock

Dawes Lane

Gdn Farm

Garden Farm

Gdn Farm

Suffolk Av

Norfolk Avenue

Oakwood Road

East Road

Avenue

Oakwood Dr

Anne Rd

Qu Anne Rd

Qu Anne Rd

Kingsmere Close

Lea Side

Gainsborough

Hogarth Close

Empress Dr

King Charles Rd

Albert Road

The Coverts

Willoughby Av

Brierley Avenue

Stable Mews

Stable Cl

East Road

Cross Way

The Cross

Beverley Avenue

Farthings Chase

Fairhaven Avenue

Empress Avenue

Seaview Avenue

Estuary Park Rd

Osborne Rd

Westwood Drive

Cross Lane

Cross Lane

Waldegraves Lane

Waldegraves Farm

Waldegraves Holiday Park

East Road

Victoria

Esplanade

Alexandra Av

East Mersea Road

Abbey Field	35 H2	Copford	32 C3	Fordstreet	22 B1	Keelers Tye	38 D4	Rush Green	
Aldham	22 A4	Copford Green	32 B5	Fox Street	19 H5	Kelvedon	52 D5	Samson's Corner	
Alresford	51 F2	Crockleford Heath	28 B2	Frinton-on-sea	54 D2	Kirby Cross	41 F4	Seven Star Green	
Ardleigh	21 G2	Crockleford Hill	27 H3	Gallows Green	22 C3	Kirby-le-Soken	41 G2	Shrub End	
Bath Side	11 F2	Dedham	6 B2	Gore Pit	53 E2	Lamb Corner	6 A5	Stanway	
Beacon End	34 A1	Dedham Heath	6 D5	Great Clacton	58 D4	Layer de la Haye	46 C5	Stanway Green	
Berechurch	47 H1	Dovercourt	11 G4	Great Holland	55 E2	Lexden	24 D4	Tiptree	
Blackheath	48 C2	East Gores	30 B3	Greenstead	37 E1	Little Tey	30 D3	Tiptree Heath	
Bocking's Elm	58 A4	Easthorpe	44 A4	Halstead	12 C2	Manningtree	8 C5	Upper Dovercourt	
Braiswick	25 E2	Eight Ash Green	23 G4	Hardy's Green	44 C4	Marks Tey	31 G3	Walton-on-the-Naze	
Brightlingsea	56 C2	Elmstead	29 F4	Harwich	11 H5	Maypole Green	47 G1	Welshwood Park	
Bromley Cross	21 H5	Elmstead Heath	39 F5	Heckfordbridge	45 G2	Mile End	18 B4	West Bergholt	
Burnt Heath	21 G4	Elmstead Market	39 G1	Hemp's Green	14 A3	Mistley	9 H5	West Mersea	
Burrsville Park	59 G2	Elmstead Row	51 G2	High Park Corner	50 B4	Old Heath	36 D4	Wivenhoe	
Cattawade	9 E2	Feering	52 C3	Holland-on-Sea	60 C4	Parkeston	10 B5		
Chitts Hills	24 A4	Fingringhoe	49 F5	Horkesley Heath	16 D2	Parson's Heath	27 E3		
Clacton-on-Sea	5 G4	Fordham	14 B3	Hurst Green	57 F4	Paternoster Heath	63 H5		
Colchester	2 A5	Fordham Heath	23 E3	The Hythe	37 E3	Rowhedge	49 F2		

USING THE STREET INDEX

Street names are listed alphabetically. Each street name is followed by its postal town or area locality, the Postcode District, the page number, and the reference to the square in which the name is found.

Standard index entries are shown as follows:

Abberton Rd *COLS* CO2...................**47** F5

Street names and selected addresses not shown on the map due to scale restrictions are shown in the index with an asterisk:

Alafin Vls *MGTR* CO11 *...................**9** E1

GENERAL ABBREVIATIONS

ACC	ACCESS	CTYD	COURTYARD	HLS	HILLS	MWY	MOTORWAY	SE	SOUT
ALY	ALLEY	CUTT	CUTTINGS	HO	HOUSE	N	NORTH	SER	SERVIC
AP	APPROACH	CV	COVE	HOL	HOLLOW	NE	NORTH EAST	SH	
AR	ARCADE	CYN	CANYON	HOSP	HOSPITAL	NW	NORTH WEST	SHOP	SHO
ASS	ASSOCIATION	DEPT	DEPARTMENT	HRB	HARBOUR	O/P	OVERPASS	SKWY	S
AV	AVENUE	DL	DALE	HTH	HEATH	OFF	OFFICE	SMT	S
BCH	BEACH	DM	DAM	HTS	HEIGHTS	ORCH	ORCHARD	SOC	S
BLDS	BUILDINGS	DR	DRIVE	HVN	HAVEN	OV	OVAL	SP	S
BND	BEND	DRO	DROVE	HWY	HIGHWAY	PAL	PALACE	SPR	S
BNK	BANK	DRY	DRIVEWAY	IMP	IMPERIAL	PAS	PASSAGE	SQ	S
BR	BRIDGE	DWGS	DWELLINGS	IN	INLET	PAV	PAVILION	ST	
BRK	BROOK	E	EAST	IND EST	INDUSTRIAL ESTATE	PDE	PARADE	STN	S
BTM	BOTTOM	EMB	EMBANKMENT	INF	INFIRMARY	PH	PUBLIC HOUSE	STR	S
BUS	BUSINESS	EMBY	EMBASSY	INFO	INFORMATION	PK	PARK	STRD	S
BVD	BOULEVARD	ESP	ESPLANADE	INT	INTERCHANGE	PKWY	PARKWAY	SW	SOUT
BY	BYPASS	EST	ESTATE	IS	ISLAND	PL	PLACE	TDG	T
CATH	CATHEDRAL	EX	EXCHANGE	JCT	JUNCTION	PLN	PLAIN	TER	TE
CEM	CEMETERY	EXPY	EXPRESSWAY	JTY	JETTY	PLNS	PLAINS	THWY	THROU
CEN	CENTRE	EXT	EXTENSION	KG	KING	PLZ	PLAZA	TNL	T
CFT	CROFT	F/O	FLYOVER	KNL	KNOLL	POL	POLICE STATION	TOLL	T
CH	CHURCH	FC	FOOTBALL CLUB	LA	LANE	PR	PRINCE	TPK	TU
CHA	CHASE	FK	FORK	LDG	LODGE	PREC	PRECINCT	TR	
CHYD	CHURCHYARD	FLD	FIELD	LGT	LIGHT	PREP	PREPARATORY	TRL	
CIR	CIRCLE	FLDS	FIELDS	LK	LOCK	PRIM	PRIMARY	TWR	
CIRC	CIRCUS	FLS	FALLS	LKS	LAKES	PROM	PROMENADE	U/P	UND
CL	CLOSE	FM	FARM	LNDG	LANDING	PRS	PRINCESS	UNI	UNIV
CLFS	CLIFFS	FT	FORT	LTL	LITTLE	PRT	PORT	UPR	
CMP	CAMP	FTS	FLATS	LWR	LOWER	PT	POINT	V	
CNR	CORNER	FWY	FREEWAY	MAG	MAGISTRATE	PTH	PATH	VA	
CO	COUNTY	FY	FERRY	MAN	MANSIONS	PZ	PIAZZA	VIAD	V
COLL	COLLEGE	GA	GATE	MD	MEAD	QD	QUADRANT	VIL	
COM	COMMON	GAL	GALLERY	MDW	MEADOWS	QU	QUEEN	VIS	
COMM	COMMISSION	GDN	GARDEN	MEM	MEMORIAL	QY	QUAY	VLG	V
CON	CONVENT	GDNS	GARDENS	MI	MILL	R	RIVER	VLS	
COT	COTTAGE	GLD	GLADE	MKT	MARKET	RBT	ROUNDABOUT	VW	
COTS	COTTAGES	GLN	GLEN	MKTS	MARKETS	RD	ROAD	W	
CP	CAPE	GN	GREEN	ML	MALL	RDG	RIDGE	WD	
CPS	COPSE	GND	GROUND	MNR	MANOR	REP	REPUBLIC	WHF	W
CR	CREEK	GRA	GRANGE	MS	MEWS	RES	RESERVOIR	WK	
CREM	CREMATORIUM	GRG	GARAGE	MSN	MISSION	RFC	RUGBY FOOTBALL CLUB	WKS	
CRS	CRESCENT	GT	GREAT	MT	MOUNT	RI	RISE	WLS	
CSWY	CAUSEWAY	GTWY	GATEWAY	MTN	MOUNTAIN	RP	RAMP	WY	
CT	COURT	GV	GROVE	MTS	MOUNTAINS	RW	ROW	YD	
CTRL	CENTRAL	HGR	HIGHER	MUS	MUSEUM	S	SOUTH	YHA	YOUTH H
CTS	COURTS	HL	HILL			SCH	SCHOOL		

POSTCODE TOWNS AND AREA ABBREVIATIONS

COL	Colchester	COS	Clacton-on-Sea	K/T/MI	Kelvedon/	RCOLE	Rural Colchester east	WOTN	Walton-on-th
COLN	Colchester north	FOS	Frinton-on-Sea		Tiptree/	RCOLW	Rural Colchester west		
COLS	Colchester south	HAR	Harwich		Mersea Island	RCOS	Rural Clacton-on-Sea		
COLW	Colchester west	HSTD	Halstead	MGTR	Manningtree	WIT	Witham		

A

		Adelaide Dr *COLS* CO2	48 B1	Albert Rd *RCOLE* CO7	57 F4	Alfred Ter *WOTN* CO14	43 E3	Amberley Cl *RCOLE* CO7	
		Adelaide St *HAR* CO12	10 C2	Albert St *COL* CO1	2 B5	Allendale Dr *RCOLW* CO6	32 C3	Ambleside Ct *COS* CO15	
Abberton Rd *COLS* CO2	47 F5	Affleck Rd *COLN* CO4	27 F5	*HAR* CO12	11 G2	Alleyne Wy *COS* CO15	64 A4	Ambrose Av *COLW* CO3	
K/T/MI CO5	49 H5	Agar Road Ap *WOTN* CO14	43 E3	Albion Gv *COLS* CO2	36 B2	Allfields *HAR* CO12	10 C5	Anchor End *MGTR* CO11	
Abbey Gate St *COL* CO1	2 C7	Agate Rd *COS* CO15	4 D5	Albion St *K/T/MI* CO5	49 H5	All Saints Av *COLW* CO3	34 D3	Anchor Hl *RCOLE* CO7	
Abbots Cl *COS* CO15	59 E3	Agincourt Rd *COS* CO15	5 A1	Albrighton Cft *COLN* CO4	18 D5	Alma St *RCOLE* CO7	50 A2	Anchor La *MGTR* CO11	
Abbots La *RCOLW* CO6	23 F5	Ainger Rd *HAR* CO12	10 B5	Aldeburgh Cl *RCOS* CO16	58 B5	Almond Cl *COS* CO15	64 C1	*RCOLE* CO7	
Abbot's Rd *COLS* CO2	36 D4	Aisne Rd *COLS* CO2	35 G3	Aldeburgh Gdns *COLN* CO4	18 C5	*K/T/MI* CO5	49 H5	Anchor Rd *COS* CO15	
Abbott Rd *HAR* CO12	10 C5	Alafin Vls *MGTR* CO11 *	9 E1	Aldercar Rd *RCOLW* CO6	45 E1	*RCOLE* CO7	38 B5	*K/T/MI* CO5	
Abdy Av *HAR* CO12	10 C5	Alamein Rd *COLS* CO2	35 F3	Alderman Howe Ldg		Almond Wy *COLN* CO4	27 F4	Andover Cl *COS* CO15	
Abels Rd *HSTD* CO9	12 C4	Alan Wy *COLW* CO3	34 C3	*COLN* CO4 *	18 C5	Alport Av *COLS* CO2	35 F3	Angel Ga *HAR* CO12 *	
Abinger Cl *RCOS* CO16	58 C3	Albany Cha *COS* CO15 *	5 J1	Alderton Rd *COLN* CO4	3 K3	Alresford Rd *RCOLE* CO7	50 D2	Angelgate Esp *HAR* CO12	
Acacia Av *COLN* CO4	27 F4	Albany Cl *RCOLW* CO6	16 B5	Ale Founder Cl *COLN* CO4	37 F1	Alston Vls *MGTR* CO11 *	9 E5	Anglefield *COS* CO15	
Accommodation Rd *COLN* CO4	17 G2	Albany Gdns East *COS* CO15	5 J1	Alexandra Av *K/T/MI* CO5	49 H5	Altbarn Cl *COLN* CO4	18 D4	Anglesea Rd *RCOLE* CO7	
Achnacone Dr *COLN* CO4	25 F1	Albany Gdns West *COS* CO15	5 J1	Alexandra Dr *RCOLE* CO7	38 B4	Altbarn Rd *COLS* CO2	37 E2	Anglia Cl *COLS* CO2	
Acland Av *COLW* CO3	24 C5	Albany Rd *RCOLW* CO6	16 C5	Alexandra Rd *COLW* CO3	2 A7	Alton Dr *COLW* CO3	35 E1	Anne Cl *RCOLE* CO7	
Acorn Av *HSTD* CO9	12 D5	Albemarle St *HAR* CO12	11 G2	*COS* CO15	4 D3	Alton Park La *COS* CO15	64 A3	Anson Cl *HAR* CO12	
Acorn Cl *COLN* CO4	19 E5	Albert Gdns *COS* CO15	5 H2	*HAR* CO12	11 G2	Alton Park Rd *COS* CO15	4 B4	Anthony Cl *COLN* CO4	
Addison Rd *FOS* CO13	54 A1	Albertine Cl *COLW* CO3	33 H1	Alexandra Ter *COLW* CO3	35 H1	Alverton Wy *COLN* CO4	26 C1	Antonius Wy *COLN* CO4	
				Alfells Rd *RCOLE* CO7	39 E1	Alyssum Wk *COLN* CO4	27 E5	Anzio Crs *COLS* CO2	

...e Cl HSTD C09 .....13 F2
...bach COS C015 .....64 A4
  ...COLS C02
...y COS C015 .....47 E1
...hambers COS C015 * 4 E4
...an COS C015 * 4 E4
...s K/T/MI C05 .....63 F3
...ids COS C015 .....59 G4
  ...COLN C04
...Cl HAR C012 .....10 C5
...rd RCOLE C07 .....21 G5
...a COLW C03 .....23 G2
...OLN C04 .....27 F5
...er MGTR C011 * 9 H5
...Wk COLS C02 .....36 B5
...Rd RCOLW C06 .....16 C5
...COLN C04 .....37 F1
...COS C015 .....1 A6
...s K/T/MI C05 .....62 D2
...s Cl COLN C04 .....3 K4
...COLS C02 .....2 D3
...COLN C04 .....27 G5
...COL C01 .....2 D7
...st COL C01 .....36 C1
...COLN C04 .....17 H5
...r RCOLW C06 .....31 G4
...S C015 .....64 C1
...COS C015 .....56 D5
...Wy COLW C04 .....27 E5
...WOTN C014 .....42 B3
...nd Cl MGTR C011 .....9 E1
...LS C02 .....48 B2
...C07 .....38 B4
...ns COLW C03 .....35 F1
...HAR C012 .....10 D4
...Gv HSTD C09 .....12 D1
...Rd FOS C013 .....55 E2
...Dr FOS C013 .....42 B5
...TD C09
...COLE C07 .....51 G2
...Cl RCOS C016 .....58 B3
...Cl K/T/MI C05 .....49 G2
...OLW C03
...Av RCOLW C06 .....32 C3
...v COLN C04 .....27 E4
...Dr COLN C04 .....18 D4
...Dr FOS C013 * 55 F2
...COS C016 .....58 C5
...1 Rd COLW C03 .....35 F2
...ns COL C01 .....36 B1
...COLN C04 .....18 C4
...d COLW C03 .....35 F2
...y FOS C013 .....42 C5
...s Cl COLN C04 .....18 C4
...COLN C04 .....58 C5
...Rd RCOS C016 .....20 C2
...ue COLW C03 .....35 H1
...C09 .....59 H2
...C07 .....50 A1
...Cl COLS C02 .....36 B5
...s COS C015 .....42 A5
...COS C015 .....52 D4
...COS C015 .....67 E3
...Rd COS C015 .....5 G2
...COLN C04 .....63 G5
...rd COS C015 .....60 D3
...rd RCOS C016 .....58 B5

B

...COLW C03 .....24 B5
...RCOLE C07 .....21 G4
...terside La RCOLE C07 .....57 E5
...owell Dr COLW C03 .....34 D4
...on RCOLW C06 .....31 F4
...on Rd COS C015 .....33 H5
...COLW C03 .....63 E4
...ge Dr K/T/MI C05 .....63 E4
  ...COLW C03
...t COL C01 .....2 B2
...a COLN C04 .....24 D3
  ...COLW C03
...COLN C04 .....37 F1
...Gdns COL C01 .....2 B6
...HI COL C01 .....2 A6
...Pas COL C01 .....2 B6
...Av COLS C02 .....48 C5
...uay Rd K/T/MI C05 .....50 A4
...OLS C02 .....18 E3
...a HSTD C09 .....11 F4
...Av COS C015 .....10 C5
...y HAR C012 .....10 C5
...Cl RCOS C016 .....58 C4
...Gdns COLS C02 .....27 G5
...k La K/T/MI C05 .....63 E2
...d Rd COLS C02 .....48 B1
...Wy FOS C013 .....42 B5
...t K/T/MI C05 .....50 B5
...MGTR C011 .....8 C5
...d Rd COLN C04 .....3 K1
...y COLW C03 .....34 A2
...ston Rd COLN C04 .....18 C4
...ct Cl COLN C04 .....26 C1
...Cl COLS C02 .....52 D3
...C011 .....9 E5
...1 Rd COLW C03 .....17 F3
...Cl COLN C04 .....33 H1
...d Ter MGTR C011 * 9 E5
...Av COLS C02 .....26 D1
...rt COLN C04 .....18 D5
...ood Wy COLS C02 .....35 G5
...La HAR C012 .....11 H3
...st COL C01 .....36 C1
...COLE C07 .....50 B5
...on Gdns COS C015 .....60 A4
...n Rd COLS C02 .....36 B2

Bateman Rd RCOLE C07 .....56 D2
Bath St RCOLE C07 .....50 A3
Bathurst Cl COLS C02 .....48 B1
Battisford Dr RCOS C016 .....58 A5
Battlesbrook Rd COLS C02 .....37 E5
Bawdsey Cl RCOS C016 .....58 B5
Bawtree Wy COLW C03 .....34 D2
Bayard Av RCOLE C07 .....57 E3
Baynards Crs FOS C013 .....42 A5
Bay Rd HAR C012 .....11 C5
Beachcroft Av FOS C013 .....41 H5
Beach Rd COS C015 .....5 F4
  HAR C012 .....11 H4
  K/T/MI C05 .....66 D4
Beacon Cl RCOLE C07 .....50 D4
Beacon Hill Av HAR C012 .....11 H5
Beaconsfield Av COLW C03 .....35 H1
Beaconsfield Rd COS C015 .....4 E3
Beacon Wy COLW C03 .....33 H1
Beatrice Rd COS C015 .....4 C5
  WOTN C014 .....43 F1
Beaumont Av COS C015 .....4 D4
  RCOLE C07 .....57 F3
Beaumont Cl COLN C04 .....17 H5
  WOTN C014 .....42 B4
Beaver Cl COLW C03 .....24 B5
Beche Rd COL C01 .....36 A3
Becker Rd COLS C02 .....34 B3
Beckford Rd MGTR C011 .....9 H5
Becontree Cl COS C015 .....59 F1
Bedford Cl K/T/MI C05 .....63 E3
Bedford Rd COLN C04 .....18 A4
  COS C015 .....59 F1
Beech Av HSTD C09 .....13 F2
Beech Cl K/T/MI C05 .....50 A1
Beech Hl COLW C03 .....34 D2
Beechwood Cl COLS C02 .....35 G5
Beehive Ct COL C01 * 36 B1
Beeleigh Cl COLS C02 .....48 B1
Begonia Pl RCOS C016 .....58 C5
Bellamy Cl FOS C013 .....41 H5
Bell Cl COLS C02 .....37 E5
Belle Vue Rd COL C01 .....2 A2
  RCOLE C07 .....50 A2
Bellfield Av RCOLE C07 .....57 E2
Bellfield Cl RCOLE C07 .....57 F3
Bellfield Rd RCOLE C07 .....57 F3
Bellingham Pl K/T/MI C05 .....52 C3
Belmont Crs COLN C04 .....26 D1
Belmont Pl COLN C04 .....36 D5
Bembridge Cl COS C015 .....59 F1
Bemerton Gdns FOS C013 .....41 G5
Benhall Cl RCOS C016 .....58 C4
Bennett Cl COL C01 .....37 F1
Bennett Cl WOTN C014 .....42 C3
Bentall Cl HSTD C09 * 13 E4
Berberis Wk COLN C04 .....27 F5
Berechurch Hall Rd COLS C02 * 47 G1
Berechurch Rd COLS C02 .....47 G1
Bergholt Rd HSTD C09 .....25 G2
  MGTR C011 .....8 C2
Beridge Rd HSTD C09 .....12 C2
Beriffe Pl RCOLE C07 .....57 E3
Berkeley Gdns K/T/MI C05 * 49 G3
Berkeley Rd COS C015 .....4 D4
Berkley Cl COLN C04 .....18 D5
Bernard Cl FOS C013 .....42 A5
Berrimans Cl COLN C04 .....37 E1
Bethany St RCOLE C07 .....50 A3
Beverley Av K/T/MI C05 .....50 B5
Beverley Dr FOS C013 .....42 A4
Beverley Rd COLW C03 .....35 G1
Bexhill Cl COS C015 .....64 C4
Bignalls Cft COLN C04 .....18 D5
Bijou Cl K/T/MI C05 .....63 E2
Bilsdale Cl COLN C04 .....18 B5
Birch Av HAR C012 .....11 E4
Birch Cl COS C015 .....64 C1
  RCOLE C07 .....56 D4
The Birches FOS C013 .....42 A5
Birch Rd COLS C02 .....46 B5
Birchwood Cl K/T/MI C05 .....63 F4
Birch Wood Cl K/T/MI C05 * 67 E4
Birchwood Wy K/T/MI C05 .....63 G3
Bird La K/T/MI C05 .....63 G5
Birkin Cl K/T/MI C05 .....62 C4
Bishop Rd COLS C02 .....34 D4
Bishops La K/T/MI C05 .....62 D1
Bisley Cl RCOS C016 * 58 B5
Bittern Cl K/T/MI C05 .....58 A5
Blackberry Rd COLW C03 .....33 H3
Blackbrook Rd RCOLW C06 .....17 F2
Blackheath COLN C04 .....48 B2
Blacksmith's La HAR C012 .....10 A5
Blackthorn Av COLN C04 .....27 F4
Blackthorn Rd HAR C012 .....10 C5
Blackwater Av COLN C04 .....48 C5
Blackwater Dr K/T/MI C05 .....66 B4
Bladon Cl K/T/MI C05 .....63 F3
Blaine Dr FOS C013 .....42 B4
Blake Cl MGTR C011 .....9 F1
Blake Dr RCOS C016 .....58 D3
Blamsters Crs HSTD C09 .....12 C4
Blanchard Cl FOS C013 .....41 E4
Bleaberry Cl COLS C02 .....48 B2
Blenheim Dr COLS C02 .....48 B1
Blenheim Rd COS C015 .....4 A5
Blenheim Wy K/T/MI C05 .....63 F4
Blind La RCOLW C06 .....23 H4
Bloom Cl FOS C013 .....42 B5
Bloomfield Av FOS C013 .....42 A4
Bluebell Av COLN C04 .....58 C5
Bluehouse Av RCOS C016 .....58 A5
Blue Rd K/T/MI C05 .....60 D3
Blyford Rd RCOS C016 .....58 B5
Blythe La RCOLE C07 * 50 A2
Boadicea Wy RCOLE C07 .....50 B2
Bobbits Wy RCOLE C07 .....50 B2
Bober Ct COLS C02 .....48 C5
Bocking's Gv RCOS C016 .....58 B4
Bois Hall Gdns HSTD C09 .....13 E2
Boley Drive COS C015 .....60 B5
Bonham Ct COS C015 .....59 G4
Booth Av COLN C04 .....3 K5
Boundary Rd COLN C04 .....37 H5
Bounstead Hl COLS C02 .....47 F5

Bounstead Rd COLS C02 .....47 G3
Bourchier Wy HSTD C09 .....12 C4
Bourne Cl HSTD C09 .....12 C4
Bournemouth Rd COS C015 .....60 D3
Bourne Rd COLS C02 .....36 B3
  RCOLW C06 .....24 B1
Bower Hall La K/T/MI C05 .....67 F1
Bowes Rd RCOLE C07 .....50 B1
Box Mill La HSTD C09 .....12 D1
Boxted Av RCOS C016 .....58 B5
Boxted Rd COLN C04 .....17 G4
Boyles Ct COLS C02 .....48 C3
The Brackens RCOLN C04 .....26 C1
Bracks La RCOLW C06 .....24 B1
Brading Av COS C015 .....59 G2
Braemore Cl COLN C04 .....27 E1
Braiswick COLN C04 .....25 E2
Braiswick La COLN C04 .....17 G5
Braithwaite Dr COLN C04 .....25 H2
Brambles WOTN C014 .....42 C4
The Brambles COLW C03 .....34 C4
Bramley Cl COLN C04 .....25 E5
  COS C015 .....51 G2
Branscombe Cl FOS C013 .....54 D1
Branston Rd COS C015 .....64 C1
Brantham Hl MGTR C011 .....8 D1
Brassingham Crs K/T/MI C05 .....50 B5
Bray Ct RCOLW C06 .....16 C5
Breachfield Rd COLS C02 .....35 F5
Bree Av RCOLW C06 .....31 F4
Brent Cl FOS C013 .....42 B4
Brentwood Rd COS C015 .....60 A3
Brereton Cl RCOS C016 .....58 B5
Brian Bishop Cl WOTN C014 .....42 D5
Briardale Av COLN C04 .....10 C4
Briarfields FOS C013 .....41 G3
Briar Rd RCOLE C07 .....21 G5
Briarwood Av COS C015 .....60 A3
Briarwood End COLN C04 .....26 C1
Brickhouse Cl K/T/MI C05 .....66 C3
Brick Kiln La RCOLW C06 .....17 E3
Brick Kiln Rd COLN C04 .....2 B1
Brickmakers La COLN C04 .....26 A2
Brick St COLW C03 .....23 G5
Bridgebrook Cl COLN C04 .....26 D1
Bridgefield Cl COL C01 .....3 K6
Bridge Hl RCOLW C06 .....14 B2
Bridge St HSTD C09 .....12 D2
The Bridleway COLW C03 .....23 F5
Brierley Av K/T/MI C05 .....67 F5
Brightlingsea Rd RCOLE C07 .....58 B5
Brighton Rd COS C015 .....60 D3
Brightside FOS C013 .....42 A4
Brindley Rd COS C015 .....59 H1
Brinkley Crs COLN C04 .....27 E2
Brinkley Grove Rd COLN C04 .....18 B4
Brinkley La COLN C04 .....26 A1
Brinkley Pl COLN C04 .....48 B1
Brisbane Wy COLS C02 .....48 B1
Bristol Rd COL C01 .....3 F4
Britannia Crs RCOLE C07 .....50 A1
Brittany Wy COS C02 .....52 D4
Britten Cl COLN C04 .....37 F1
Brixham Cl COS C015 .....64 C4
Broadfields RCOLE C07 .....38 B5
Broadlands Wy COLN C04 .....27 F3
Broadmead Rd COLN C04 .....27 E3
Broadmere Cl COS C015 .....4 D3
Broad Oaks Pk COLN C04 .....27 E1
Brock Cl K/T/MI C05 .....63 F2
Brockham Cl RCOS C016 .....58 B3
Brockwell La K/T/MI C05 .....52 C5
Bromley Cl RCOS C016 .....58 B5
Bromley Rd COLN C04 .....27 F3
  RCOLE C07 .....50 A2
Brook Cl K/T/MI C05 .....63 G5
Brook Farm Cl HSTD C09 .....13 F3
Brook Hall Rd K/T/MI C05 .....50 A4
Brookland K/T/MI C05 .....62 D4
Brooklands COL C01 .....2 A5
Brooklands Ri MGTR C011 .....9 E1
Brooklands Rd WOTN C014 .....8 D2
Brooklyn Ms HAR C012 * 11 F4
Brooklyn Rd HAR C012 .....11 F4
Brook Mdw K/T/MI C05 .....62 D4
Brook Rd K/T/MI C05 .....63 G5
  RCOLW C06 .....22 D5
Brookside Cl COLS C02 .....36 C3
Brooks Malting MGTR C011 * 9 E5
Brook St COL C01 .....3 G6
  MGTR C011 .....9 E5
  RCOLE C07 .....50 A2
  RCOLW C06 .....16 B5
Broome Gv WOTN C014 .....38 A5
Broomfield Crs RCOLE C07 .....38 A5
Broomhills Rd K/T/MI C05 .....67 E4
Broton Dr HSTD C09 .....12 D2
Brougham Glades COLW C03 .....34 A2
Broughton Cl COLS C02 .....34 C1
Browning Cl COS C015 .....34 C1
Browning Rd MGTR C011 .....8 D2
Brownsea Wy COLW C03 .....34 D3
Bruff Cl COLN C04 .....25 H2
Bruff Dr WOTN C014 .....42 C4
Brunel Cl COLN C04 .....59 H1
Brunel Rd COS C015 .....59 H1
Brunel Wy COLS C02 .....18 D3
Bryanstone Ms FOS C013 .....34 B2
Buckfast Av FOS C013 .....41 H5
Buckingham Dr COLN C04 .....27 F5
Buddleia Ct RCOLE C07 .....50 A3
Buffett Wy COLN C04 .....37 F1
Bullace Cl COLN C04 .....27 E1
Bullfinch Cl COLN C04 .....27 G4
Bullfinch Dr HSTD C09 .....13 F3
Bull Hill Rd COLN C04 .....59 H4
Bullock Wood Cl COLN C04 .....19 E5
Burgate Rd RCOS C016 .....58 A5
Burlington Rd COLW C03 .....2 A7
Burmanny Cl COS C015 .....64 C1
Burnham Ct WOTN C014 .....42 D3
Burnham Ct COS C015 .....64 C4
Burns Av COLW C03 .....34 C2

Burnt Heath Cottages
  RCOLE C07 .....21 F5
Burrows Cl MGTR C011 .....8 C5
Burrs Rd COS C015 .....59 G4
Burstall Cl RCOS C016 .....58 B5
Bury Cl COL C01 .....3 F4
  COS C015 .....31 C4
Burywoods COLN C04 .....25 F3
Bushell Wy COS C015 .....42 A5
Butchers La WOTN C014 .....42 A5
Butler Rd HSTD C09 .....12 C2
Butt Rd COLS C02 .....35 G2
Buxey Cl K/T/MI C05 .....66 C3
Buxton Rd COLS C02 .....36 B4
Byron Av COLW C03 .....24 C5

C

Cadenhouse Ms COLW C03 .....24 B5
Cairns Rd COLS C02 .....36 B5
California Cl COLN C04 .....18 C5
California Rd MGTR C011 .....9 H5
Cambrai Rd COLS C02 .....35 G2
Cambridge Rd COLW C03 .....35 G2
  COS C015 .....4 D1
  FOS C013 .....55 G1
Camellia Av RCOS C016 .....58 C5
Camellia Crs RCOS C016 .....58 C5
Camomile Wy COLN C04 .....25 F2
Campbell Dr COLN C04 .....27 F2
Camperwell Cl RCOLE C07 .....57 E2
Campion Rd COLN C04 .....25 F2
Camulodunum Wy COLS C02 .....47 F1
Camulus Cl COLS C02 .....34 D5
Canberra Cl COLS C02 .....48 B1
Canning St HAR C012 .....11 G2
Cannon Rd COL C01 .....2 E7
Cannons Cl COLS C02 .....35 G2
Canonium Ms K/T/MI C05 .....52 C4
Canterbury Rd COS C015 .....60 C4
  COS C015 .....60 C4
Canwick Gv COLS C02 .....36 D3
Cape Cl COLW C03 .....42 A4
Capel Pk FOS C013 .....42 A4
Capel Rd COLW C03 .....35 F2
Cap Pillar Cl RCOLE C07 .....38 A5
Capstan Pl COLN C04 .....37 E2
Captains Rd K/T/MI C05 .....66 C4
Caracalla Wy COLN C04 .....18 B3
Cardinal Cl COLN C04 .....18 B3
Carisbrooke Av COS C015 .....59 G2
Carlisle Cl COL C01 .....3 F5
Carlton Rd COS C015 .....59 H5
Carnarvon Rd COS C015 .....4 E5
Carolina Wy K/T/MI C05 .....63 F2
Caroline Cl RCOLE C07 .....38 B4
Caroline Ct COLS C02 * 34 D4
Carriers Cl K/T/MI C05 .....66 B3
Carrington Dr K/T/MI C05 .....50 A4
Carringtons Rd RCOLE C07 .....21 G5
Carrs Rd COS C015 .....59 G4
Carshalton End COLW C03 .....34 A2
Cartbridge Cl WOTN C014 .....42 D3
Carters Cl RCOS C016 .....64 B1
Cassino Rd COLS C02 .....35 F4
Castle Bailey COL C01 * 2 C5
Castlegate St HAR C012 * 11 H1
Castle Hl RCOLE C07 .....6 C5
Castle Hill Pk COS C015 * 59 F2
Castle Rd COL C01 .....2 E4
  RCOLE C07 .....50 D2
Castleward Cl RCOLE C07 .....50 D2
Catchpool Rd COL C01 .....2 C2
Caterham Cl RCOLE C07 .....50 D4
Catherine Cl COS C015 .....59 F1
Catherine Hunt Wy COLS C02 .....35 E5
Cattawade St MGTR C011 .....8 D2
Cattermole Cl RCOS C016 .....64 B1
Causeway End MGTR C011 * 8 C2
Causeway Reach RCOS C016 .....59 E2
The Causeway COLN C04 .....12 D3
  HSTD C09 .....12 D3
Cavalry Barracks COLS C02 * 35 G2
Cavendish Av COLS C02 .....35 G2
Cavendish Dr RCOS C016 .....58 A5
Caxton Cl COLN C04 .....18 D3
Cedar Av K/T/MI C05 .....66 C3
  RCOLE C07 .....56 C3
Cedar Cl WOTN C014 .....42 D3
Cedar Dr COLN C04 .....27 E1
Cedars Rd COLS C02 .....2 B7
Celandine Ct COLN C04 .....25 F2
Centaury Ct COLW C03 .....33 H3
Central Wy WOTN C014 .....42 C5
Central Maltings MGTR C011 * 9 E5
Central Pde COS C015 * 4 D4
The Centre HSTD C09 .....12 D2
Centurion Wy COLS C02 .....34 D5
Chaffinch Gdns COLN C04 .....27 G5
Chaffinch Wy HSTD C09 .....13 F3
Chalfont Rd COLN C04 .....26 C1
Challenge Wy WOTN C014 .....42 C5
Chamberlain Av WOTN C014 .....42 D5
Chancery Gv COLS C02 .....48 B2
Chandlers Ct RCOS C016 .....64 A3
Chandlers Rw COL C01 .....36 C2
Chaney Rd RCOLE C07 .....37 H5
Chanterelle COLN C04 .....26 C1
Chantry Cl COS C015 .....59 E2
The Chantry COLW C03 .....24 A3
Chapel Ct RCOLE C07 .....20 D2
Chapel Cut MGTR C011 .....9 H5
Chapelfields FOS C013 .....55 F5
Chapel Hl HSTD C09 .....12 C2
Chapel La RCOLE C07 .....28 A3
  RCOLE C07 .....50 D3
  RCOLW C06 .....16 B5
Chapel Rd COLW C03 .....33 H1

  K/T/MI C05 .....63 F4
  RCOLE C07 .....50 A2
  RCOLE C07 .....57 F4
  .....24 A1
Chapel St HSTD C09 .....12 D2
  .....49 G2
Chapel St North COL C01 .....2 B7
Chapel St South COLS C02 .....2 B7
Chaplin Dr COLN C04 .....27 E3
Chaplins FOS C013 .....42 B4
Chapman Rd COS C015 .....4 E3
Chapmans La K/T/MI C05 .....67 C1
Chapel Rd RCOLW C06 .....14 C2
Charles Peil Rd COLN C04 .....37 F1
Charles Pell Rd RCOLE C07 .....57 E4
Charles St COL C01 .....36 B1
Charlotte Dr FOS C013 .....42 A5
Charnock Cl FOS C013 .....42 B5
Charter Ct COLN C04 .....18 D5
Charter Wy COLN C04 .....17 H5
Chartfield Dr FOS C013 .....41 H5
Chase Ct COLN C04 .....27 F5
Chase La HAR C012 .....10 B5
The Chase COLW C03 * 34 B1
  COS C015 .....60 D4
  K/T/MI C05 .....66 D4
  RCOLE C07 .....6 D5
  RCOLE C07 .....39 G1
  RCOS C016 .....22 A4
The Chase Wy COLW C03 .....25 F5
Chatsworth Gdns COS C015 .....43 A5
Chatsworth Rd K/T/MI C05 .....66 D3
Chaucer Cl COLN C04 .....64 A3
Chaucer Wy COLW C03 .....24 C5
Chelmer Cl FOS C013 .....42 A4
Chelmsford Rd COS C015 .....60 A3
The Chequers RCOLE C07 .....9 F5
Cherry Cha K/T/MI C05 .....63 E4
Cherry Rw COLW C03 .....34 C2
Cherry Tree Av COS C015 .....64 C3
Cherry Tree Cl HSTD C09 .....13 F2
Cherry Tree La COLS C02 .....48 B4
Cherrywood Dr COLW C03 .....34 C2
Chervil Cl K/T/MI C05 .....62 D4
Chestnut Av COLS C02 .....48 B2
  COS C015 .....64 A2
  FOS C013 .....41 G5
Chestnut Rd RCOLE C07 * 51 G2
Chestnut Wy K/T/MI C05 .....50 D2
  RCOLE C07 .....56 D5
Cheveling Rd COLS C02 .....37 E5
Chilburn Rd COS C015 .....59 F2
Childwell Aly COL C01 .....2 E7
Chiltern Cl COLN C04 .....17 E2
Chilton Cl RCOLW C06 .....17 G2
Chingford Av COS C015 .....59 F1
Chinook COLN C04 .....18 C5
Chippetts La COLW C03 .....22 B5
Chipping Hl HSTD C09 .....13 E2
Chipstead Wk RCOS C016 .....58 C5
Chittock Cl RCOS C016 .....64 B1
Chitts Hl COLW C03 .....23 E3
Choats Wd COLW C03 .....34 A3
Christ Church Ct COLW C03 .....35 G2
Christine Cha COLW C03 .....34 C2
Church Cl RCOLW C06 .....16 B5
Church Cnr RCOLE C07 * 22 A4
Church Crs COS C015 .....5 F4
Church Farm Wy COS C015 .....17 H5
Churchfield Rd WOTN C014 .....43 E3
Churchfields K/T/MI C05 .....66 C4
Church Gv RCOLW C06 .....33 H5
Church Hi K/T/MI C05 .....22 A4
Churchill Av HSTD C09 .....13 F1
Churchill Cl RCOLE C07 .....57 E2
Churchill Rd COS C015 .....63 G5
Churchill Wy COLS C02 .....36 C3
Church La COLW C03 .....34 C1
  COS C015 .....54 B3
  MGTR C011 .....9 H5
  RCOLW C06 .....30 A4
  RCOLW C06 .....31 H5
Church Rd COS C015 .....5 C4
  K/T/MI C05 .....62 D3
  K/T/MI C05 .....66 C4
  RCOLE C07 .....39 F1
  RCOLE C07 .....51 G3
  RCOLE C07 .....56 D2
  RCOLW C06 .....14 C4
  RCOLW C06 .....23 E3
Church St COL C01 .....2 B6
  HAR C012 .....11 G1
  K/T/MI C05 .....49 G2
  RCOLW C06 .....16 B5
Church Vw RCOLE C07 .....20 D2
Church Wk COL C01 .....2 B6
Churnwood Rd COLN C04 .....27 E3
Cinque Port Rd RCOLE C07 .....57 E5
Circular Rd East COLS C02 .....36 A2
Circular Rd North COLS C02 .....35 H2
Circular Rd South COLS C02 .....35 H3
Circular Rd West COLS C02 .....35 H2
City Rd K/T/MI C05 .....66 B5
Clacton Rd FOS C013 .....54 A5
  RCOLE C07 .....58 B2
Claire Rd FOS C013 .....54 A5
Clairmont Rd COLW C03 .....34 B2
Clara Reeve Cl COLW C03 .....34 C3
Clare St HSTD C09 .....12 D5
Claremont Hts COL C01 .....2 A1
Claremont Rd RCOLE C07 .....50 B2
Clarendon Pk COS C015 .....59 H4
Clarendon Wy COL C01 .....2 B2
Clarkes Rd HAR C012 .....11 G5
Clarkesmead K/T/MI C05 .....62 D4
Clarkia Wk COLN C04 .....27 F5
Claudius Rd COLS C02 .....36 B2
Clayhall Rd COS C015 .....59 G4
Clay Lane Gv COLN C04 .....19 E5

Clays Rd WOTN CO14.....42 C3
Clearwater COLS CO2.....36 C3
Clematis Wy COLN CO4.....27 F5
Cleveland Cl COLN CO4.....18 D5
Cliff Pde WOTN CO14.....43 G1
Cliff Rd COS CO15.....60 C4
 HAR CO12.....11 F5
Cliff Wy COS CO15.....55 C1
Clifton Ter RCOLE CO7.....50 A2
Clive Rd COLS CO2.....36 A2
Cloes La RCOS CO16.....58 B5
The Cloisters K/T/MI CO5.....52 B5
The Close COS CO15.....64 A5
 FOS CO13.....54 A3
 FOS CO13.....55 E1
 HAR CO12.....10 D4
Clough Rd COLN CO4.....18 D3
Cloverlands COLN CO4.....3 K1
Clovers HSTD CO9.....12 C3
Clover Wy RCOLE CO7.....9 E4
Coach Rd COS CO15.....51 G3
 RCOLW CO6.....16 B1
Coan Av COS CO15.....4 B7
Coats Hutton Rd COLS CO2.....35 E4
Cockaynes La RCOLE CO7.....51 F1
Coeur De Lion COLN.....26 A2
Coggeshall Rd RCOLW CO6.....36 B4
Coggeshall Wy HSTD CO9.....13 F2
Cohort Dr COLS CO2.....34 D5
Coke St HAR CO12.....11 G2
Colchester Rd COLN CO4.....37 H2
 COS CO15.....60 A4
 HSTD CO9.....13 E3
 K/T/MI CO5.....63 E1
 K/T/MI CO5.....66 D1
 RCOLE CO7.....6 B4
 RCOLE CO7.....20 B3
 RCOLE CO7.....38 A5
 RCOLW CO6.....15 H1
Coles La WOTN CO14.....42 C2
College Rd COS CO15.....5 C2
Coller Rd HAR CO12.....11 G2
Collindale Gdns COS CO15.....60 A4
Collingwood Rd RCOLW CO6.....34 B1
 COS CO15.....4 B7
Colne Bank Av COL CO1.....2 A3
Colne Cswy COLS CO2.....37 E2
Colne Ri K/T/MI CO5.....49 G2
Colne Rd COS CO15.....4 B5
 HSTD CO9.....13 F2
 RCOLE CO7.....56 D4
Colne Valley Cl HSTD CO9.....12 C2
Colthorpe Rd COS CO15.....59 F1
Coltsfoot Ct COLN CO4.....25 F2
Columbine Gdns WOTN CO14.....42 D4
Columbine Ms COLN CO4.....23 H5
Colvin Cl COLW CO3.....34 C1
Commerce Pk COLS CO2.....37 E3
Commerce Wy COLS CO2.....37 E4
 MGTR CO11.....8 D4
The Commons COLN CO4.....3 J5
Compton Ms COLN CO4.....34 D3
Compton Rd COLN CO4.....3 J4
Conder Wy COLS CO2.....36 D3
Conies HSTD CO9.....12 C5
Conifer Cl COLN CO4.....27 E4
 RCOLE CO7.....51 E5
Connaught Av FOS CO13.....55 E5
Connaught Cl COS CO15.....5 K2
Connaught Gdns East
 COS CO15.....5 J1
Connaught Gdns West
 COS CO15.....5 J1
Constable Av COS CO16.....58 C3
Constable Cl COLN CO4.....17 H5
 K/T/MI CO5.....67 E3
 MGTR CO11.....8 C5
Constable Rw RCOLE CO7 *.....6 D5
Constantine Rd COLW CO3.....35 G2
Conway Cl HSTD CO9.....13 F2
 RCOLE CO7.....50 B2
Cook Crs COLN CO4.....27 F5
Cooks Cl HSTD CO9.....13 E4
Cook's Hall Rd RCOLW CO6.....23 H1
Cook's La COLW CO3.....24 B4
Coolyne Wy COS CO15.....59 H2
Coopers Crs RCOLW CO6.....16 C5
Coopers La COS CO15.....64 C1
 RCOLE CO7.....50 A1
Cooper Wk COLN CO4.....27 E4
Coppens Rd RCOLE CO7.....57 E5
Copper Beeches COLW CO3.....34 A2
Coppice End RCOLN CO4.....26 C1
Coppice Rd COLS CO2.....58 C3
The Coppice COS CO15.....4 B7
Coppingford End RCOLW CO6.....32 C2
Coppins Rd COS CO15.....59 F4
The Copse COLN CO4.....26 A1
Coralin Wk COLW CO3.....33 H1
Coriander Rd K/T/MI CO5.....62 D4
Cornell Cl K/T/MI CO5.....62 D5
Cornflower Cl COLW CO3.....23 H5
Cornflower Rd COS CO15.....64 A5
Cornford Wy MGTR CO11 *.....8 C5
Cornwallis Dr RCOLW CO6.....31 F4
Coronation Av COLW CO3.....42 B1
Coronation Rd COS CO15.....59 F4
Corporation Yd COLN CO4 *.....3 J3
Cortoncroft Cl FOS CO15.....42 B4
Cotman Av MGTR CO11.....8 C4
Cotman Rd COS CO15.....58 D3
 RCOS CO16.....58 D3
Cotswold Ct COLN CO4.....18 D5
Cotswold Rd COS CO15.....59 F4
Cottage Dr COLS CO2.....36 D4
Cottage Gn COS CO15.....58 C3
Cottage Gv RCOS CO16.....58 B5
Cottage Wk RCOS CO16.....58 B5
Cottonwood Cl COLS CO2.....58 C3
Coulsdon Cl RCOS CO16.....58 C3
Courtauld Cl HSTD CO9.....13 F2
The Courtyards COLN CO4 *.....18 D5
Coventry Cl COL CO1.....2 E6
The Coverts K/T/MI CO5.....67 E4
Cowdray Av COL CO1.....2 C2

Cowdray Crs COL CO1.....2 D6
Cowslip Ct COLW CO3.....23 H5
Cox Rd RCOLE CO7.....51 G2
Crabtree FOS CO15.....41 G3
Cracknell Rd RCOLE CO7.....38 A5
Craigfield Av COS CO15.....59 F3
Cranborne Cl COLN CO4.....26 A2
Crane Av COLW CO3.....33 C5
Cranford Cl FOS CO15.....55 E1
Cranleigh Cl COS CO16.....58 B3
Craven Dr COLN CO4.....18 D5
Credon Cl COS CO15.....59 F2
Credon Dr COS CO15.....59 F2
Creekhurst Cl RCOLE CO7.....57 F4
Creffield Rd COLS CO2.....35 G1
Crescent Rd WOTN CO14.....43 E3
The Crescent COLN CO4.....18 D2
 COS CO15.....59 H2
 COS CO15.....55 F1
 RCOLW CO6.....16 A4
 RCOLW CO6.....31 H4
Crestlands RCOLE CO7.....51 C3
Croft Rd COS CO15.....4 B1
 K/T/MI CO5.....52 B4
Crome Cl COLN CO4.....34 D2
Crome Rd RCOS CO16.....58 C3
Cromwell Rd COL CO1.....58 A1
Crooked Elms HAR CO12.....11 F4
Croquet Gdns RCOLE CO7.....50 B1
Crossfield Rd COS CO15.....4 D2
Crossfield Wy COS CO13.....41 F5
Cross La K/T/MI CO5.....52 A4
Crosstree Wks COLS CO2.....56 B4
Cross Wy K/T/MI CO5.....67 F3
Crouch St COLW CO3.....2 A7
Crowhurst Rd COLW CO3.....2 A6
Crown Bays Rd COLN CO4.....3 K3
Crown Ct COLN CO4 *.....18 D3
Crown Ga COLN CO4.....19 E3
Crown La HAR CO12.....11 G3
Crown La North RCOLE CO7.....19 F2
Crown La South RCOLE CO7.....19 H5
Crown Rd COS CO15.....64 C3
Crown St RCOLE CO7.....6 C3
Culver Sq COL CO1 *.....2 B6
Culver St East COL CO1.....2 D6
Culver St West COL CO1.....2 B6
Culver Wk COL CO1 *.....2 C6
Cunobelin Wy COLS CO2.....34 D5
Curlew Cl COS CO15.....59 H3
 K/T/MI CO5.....52 D4
Curlew Cft COLN CO4.....27 G4
Currents La HAR CO12.....11 G1
Curtis Cl RCOS CO16.....64 B1
The Cut K/T/MI CO5.....62 D5
Cutting Dr HSTD CO9.....12 D3
Cygnet Wk COLW CO3.....33 G3
Cymbeline Wy
 (Colchester By-Pass)
 COLW CO3.....24 C5
Cypress Cl COS CO15.....59 E2
Cypress Gv COLW CO3.....27 F4
Cypress Ms K/T/MI CO5.....66 C3
Cyril Child Cl COLN CO4.....27 F5

D

Dahlia Cl RCOS CO16.....58 D3
Dahlia Wk RCOS CO16.....27 E5
Daisy Green Rd COLW CO3.....22 C4
Dale Cl COLW CO3.....23 C5
Dale Rd HAR CO12.....10 D5
The Dale RCOLE CO7.....50 B2
Damant's Farm La FOS CO15.....40 B3
Damask Rd COLW CO3.....23 H5
Daniel Cole Rd COLS CO2.....36 A3
Daniell Cl RCOS CO16.....58 C3
Daniell Dr COLS CO2.....35 E1
D'Arcy Cl FOS CO13.....42 E5
D'Arcy Hts COLS CO2.....36 D4
D'Arcy Rd COLS CO2.....63 C5
D'Arcy Wy RCOLE CO7.....56 D3
Darina Ct COLW CO3 *.....23 C5
Darkhouse La K/T/MI CO5.....49 H2
Darnel Wy COLW CO3.....23 G5
Darwin Cl COLS CO2.....48 C1
Davey Cl COL CO1.....3 K7
Davy Rd COS CO15.....60 A1
Dawes La K/T/MI CO5.....67 H5
Dawlish Rd COS CO15.....64 C4
Dawnford Cl COLW CO3.....33 H1
Dazeley's La RCOLE CO7.....8 A1
Dead La RCOLE CO7.....20 B1
Deal Cl COS CO15.....64 C4
Deal Wy RCOLE CO7.....50 B2
Deanes's Cl HAR CO12.....10 D5
Deanes Ct HAR CO12.....10 D5
Deanhill Av COS CO15.....59 H4
Dean St RCOLE CO7.....50 B2
Deben Rd COS CO15.....59 H4
Deben Wk RCOS CO16.....58 B5
De Burgh Rd COLW CO3.....34 B1
Dedham Av RCOS CO16.....58 B5
Dedham Mdw RCOLE CO7 *.....6 C2
Dedham Rd MGTR CO11.....7 H5
 RCOLE CO7.....6 C1
Deepdale Rd HAR CO12.....10 C5
Defoe Crs COLN CO4.....17 H4
Delamere Rd COLN CO4.....27 E1
Delius Wk K/T/MI CO5.....37 H1
Delia Cl COLW CO3 *.....35 G1
The Dell COL CO1.....2 A7
Denham Ct RCOLE CO7.....50 B2
Dereham Cl COLS CO2.....35 F4
Derwent Gdns COS CO15.....60 A3
Derwent Rd COLN CO4.....18 D4
De Staunton Cl RCOLE CO7.....51 G3
Devereaux Cl WOTN CO14.....42 B3
Devereaux Pl COLN CO4.....25 F1
De Vere Cl RCOLE CO7.....50 A2
De Vere La RCOLE CO7.....50 A2

De Vere Rd COLW CO3.....34 C2
De Veres Rd HSTD CO9 *.....12 C3
De Vere Wy HAR CO12.....10 C5
Devon Rd COS CO15.....35 E4
Devon Wy COS CO15.....60 C2
 HAR CO12.....10 A5
Dewberry Cl COLN CO4.....27 E5
Diana Wy COS CO15.....64 C2
Dilbridge Rd East COLN CO4.....3 J3
Dilbridge Rd West COLN CO4.....3 H3
Dinants Crs RCOLW CO6.....31 F4
Dinsdale Cl COLN CO4.....3 K4
Distillery La COLS CO2.....36 D3
Dixon Av RCOS CO16.....64 A4
Dixon Cl MGTR CO11.....8 C5
Dixon Wy RCOLE CO7.....37 H4
Dobbies La RCOLW CO6.....31 G4
Dockfield Av HAR CO12.....10 C4
Docwra Pl K/T/MI CO5 *.....52 C4
Docwra Rd K/T/MI CO5.....52 C4
Doggetts La RCOLW CO6.....31 G5
Domitian Cl COLN CO4.....18 C4
Domsey Bank RCOLW CO6.....31 H1
Donard Dr RCOLW CO6.....16 A5
Donne Dr COS CO15.....64 A4
Donyland Wy K/T/MI CO5.....49 E3
Dooley Rd HSTD CO9.....12 C3
Dorchester End COLS CO2.....36 C4
Dorking Crs RCOS CO16.....58 C3
Dorothy Curtice Ct
 RCOLW CO6.....32 D2
Dorset Cl COS CO15.....60 C3
Douglas Rd COS CO15.....58 D5
 HAR CO12.....11 E3
Dove Crs HAR CO12.....10 D5
Dovedale Gdns COS CO15.....60 A3
Dover Cl COS CO15.....64 D4
Dover Rd RCOLE CO7.....57 E3
Dowches Dr K/T/MI CO5.....52 C3
Dowches Gdns K/T/MI CO5.....52 C3
Drakes Ap COS CO15.....64 A3
Driffield Cl K/T/MI CO5.....52 C4
The Drive COS CO15.....59 H2
 HAR CO12.....11 E5
Drury Rd COLS CO2.....35 F2
Dry Dock RCOLE CO7.....50 A2
Dudley Cl COLS CO2.....36 B3
Dudley Rd COS CO15.....4 B2
Duffield Dr COLN CO4.....27 F5
Dugard Av COLW CO3.....34 B3
Duke St RCOLE CO7.....56 D4
Dulwich Rd COS CO15.....60 B4
Duncan Rd COS CO15.....52 C4
Dunlin Ct K/T/MI CO5.....52 C4
Dunnock Wy COLN CO4.....27 F5
Dunthorne Rd COS CO15.....59 H3
Dunthorpe Rd RCOS CO16.....58 D3
Dupont Cl RCOS CO16.....58 D3
Durham Sq COL CO1.....3 F5
Dyer's Rd COLN CO4.....33 H4

E

Eagle Av WOTN CO14.....43 F2
Eaglegate COL CO1 *.....3 F5
Earlhams Cl HAR CO12.....10 C5
Earlswood Wy COLS CO2.....35 G5
East Bay COL CO1.....3 G6
Eastcliff Av COS CO15.....59 H5
East Dock Rd HAR CO12.....10 C1
Easterford Rd K/T/MI CO5.....52 C4
Easterling Cl HAR CO12.....10 D5
Eastern Rd RCOLE CO7.....56 D4
East Gores Rd RCOLW CO6.....59 E4
Easthaven COS CO15.....59 E4
East Hl COL CO1.....3 F5
Easthorpe Rd K/T/MI CO5.....44 A2
East La RCOLE CO7.....6 B4
East Mersea Rd K/T/MI CO5.....67 H1
Easton Wy FOS CO13.....42 E5
East Rd K/T/MI CO5.....67 E3
East Stockwell St COL CO1.....3 F5
East St COL CO1.....3 H5
 HAR CO12.....11 G3
East Ter WOTN CO14.....43 F2
East Vw RCOLE CO7 *.....20 B1
East Ward Ms COL CO1.....3 J5
Eaton Ms COLS CO2.....36 C4
Ebony Cl COS CO15.....33 G5
Edenside FOS CO15.....42 B4
Edgware Rd RCOS CO16.....58 D4
Edison Gdns COLN CO4.....3 J2
Edison Rd COS CO15.....60 C3
Edith Rd COS CO15.....4 D5
 FOS CO13.....41 H3
Edward Av RCOLE CO7.....57 E3
Edward St HAR CO12.....10 B2
Egerton Green Rd COLS CO2.....34 D4
Egremont Wy COLN CO4.....33 H3
Egret Crs COLW CO3.....27 H4
Eight Acre La COLS CO2.....33 F5
Eld La COL CO1.....2 C6
Eldon Cl COLN CO4.....27 F3
Eldred Av COS CO15.....35 E4
Eleanor Cl K/T/MI CO5.....65 E2
Elianore Rd COLW CO3.....35 E5
Elizabeth Cl COLN CO4.....18 C5
Elizabeth Rd HAR CO12.....10 D4
Elizabeth Wy HSTD CO9.....12 D2
 RCOLE CO7.....50 B2
Elliots Dr WOTN CO14.....42 D5
Ellis Rd COS CO15.....4 D5
Elm Cl K/T/MI CO5.....67 E3
 RCOLE CO7.....51 G2
Elm Crs COLN CO4.....27 E3
Elmcroft RCOLE CO7.....39 E1
Elmdale Dr MGTR CO11.....9 E5

Elmden Ct COS CO15.....59 E4
Elm Dr HAR CO12.....11 E4
 HSTD CO9.....13 E3
 RCOLE CO7.....56 C3
Elmfield Cl COS CO15.....60 C2
Elm Gv COS CO15.....59 E5
 COS CO15.....64 A2
 COS CO15.....41 G5
Elmhurst Rd HAR CO12.....11 F4
Elmstead Rd COLN CO4.....37 E1
 RCOLE CO7.....38 C3
The Elms FOS CO13 *.....55 F1
Elm Ter MGTR CO11 *.....9 E5
Elm Tree Av K/T/MI CO5.....42 B4
Elm Tree Cl COS CO15.....42 B5
Elmwood Av COLS CO2.....35 E5
Elthorne Pk RCOS CO16.....58 D5
Elwes Cl COLN CO4.....27 E5
Elwin Rd K/T/MI CO5.....63 E3
Empire Rd HAR CO12.....11 G3
Empress Av K/T/MI CO5.....67 E3
Empress Dr K/T/MI CO5.....67 E4
Endean Ct RCOLE CO7.....37 H5
Endsleigh Ct COLW CO3.....25 C5
Enid Wy COLN CO4.....25 F2
Enville Wy COS CO15.....18 C5
Epping Cl COS CO15.....59 F1
Epsom Cl RCOS CO16.....58 C3
Erica Wk COLN CO4.....27 E5
Erle Havard Rd
 RCOLW CO6.....16 B5
Ernest Rd RCOLE CO7.....50 B1
Errington Rd COLW CO3.....35 G2
Erskine Rd MGTR CO11.....9 E5
Esplanade FOS CO13.....55 F3
The Esplanade COS CO15.....61 G3
Essex Hall Rd COL CO1.....2 C4
Essex Wy HAR CO12.....11 F5
 RCOLE CO7.....8 A5
Essex Yeomanry Wy
 COLW CO3.....23 G5
Estuary Cl COLN CO4.....17 H5
Estuary Crs COS CO15.....4 B5
Estuary Park Rd K/T/MI CO5.....49 H2
Eton Rd COS CO15.....4 E1
 FOS CO13.....55 G1
Eudo Rd COLS CO2.....35 F3
Europa Wy HAR CO12.....10 A5
Evergreen Dr COLN CO4.....19 E5
Ewan Cl COLW CO3.....33 H1
Ewan Wy COLW CO3.....33 H1
Ewell Hall Cha K/T/MI CO5.....52 C5
Exeter Cl RCOLW CO6.....17 E2
Exeter Dr COL CO1.....3 F5

F

Factory Hl K/T/MI CO5.....63 F5
Factory La MGTR CO11.....8 D2
Factory La East HSTD CO9.....12 D3
Factory La West HSTD CO9.....12 D3
Fair Cl RCOLE CO7.....57 F4
Fairclough Av RCOS CO16.....64 B1
Fairfax Rd COL CO1.....36 A1
Fairfield Gdns COLN CO4.....4 D2
Fairfield Rd COS CO15.....59 F4
Fairhaven Av K/T/MI CO5.....67 F3
Fairhead Rd North
 COLN CO4.....3 J3
Fairhead Rd South
 COLN CO4.....3 J5
Fairlop Cl COS CO15.....59 F1
Fairways COLN CO4.....25 E1
Falcon Crs COL CO1.....36 C2
Falcon Wy COS CO15.....59 F3
Falcon Yd RCOLE CO7.....50 B2
Falklands Dr MGTR CO11.....9 E5
Fallowfield Cl HAR CO12.....10 C4
Fallowfield Rd COS CO15.....35 F5
Faraday Cl COS CO15.....59 G1
Farmers Wy RCOS CO16.....64 B1
Farmleigh Av COS CO15.....59 F1
Farm Wk RCOLE CO7.....56 D2
Farriers End COLW CO3.....34 A2
Farrington Cl COL CO1.....3 K7
Farthings Cha K/T/MI CO5.....67 F3
Feedhams Cl K/T/MI CO5.....67 F4
Fering Hl K/T/MI CO5.....52 D3
Felixstowe Cl RCOS CO16.....58 A5
Fellowes Cl COLN CO4.....26 A2
Felstead Ct COLS CO2.....48 B2
Fen Br RCOLE CO7.....7 E1
Fenbridge La RCOLE CO7.....7 E1
Fennell Cl K/T/MI CO5.....62 D5
Fenno Cl COLW CO3.....34 B3
Fenn Rd HSTD CO9.....13 F2
Ferndale Cl COS CO15.....59 F2
Ferndale Rd HAR CO12.....11 G2
Fernhall La COLN CO4.....26 A2
Fernlea Cl COLN CO4.....25 F2
Fernlea Rd HAR CO12.....11 G2
Fernwood Av COS CO15.....60 D4
Ferry Rd K/T/MI CO5.....50 D4
Fiddlers Folly COLW CO3.....22 D5
Fiddlers Hl COLW CO3.....22 D5
Fieldview Cl COLN CO4.....18 A5
Field Wy RCOLE CO7.....38 B5
Fifth Av FOS CO13.....55 E1
 HSTD CO9.....13 C3
Finchdale COS CO15.....59 F5
Finchingfield Wy COLS CO2.....48 B2
Finer Ct RCOS CO16.....64 B1
Fingringhoe Rd COLS CO2.....37 E5
 RCOLE CO7.....49 E1
Finham Cl COLN CO4.....27 E5
Finsbury Pl HSTD CO9 *.....13 E2
Firlie Wk COS CO15.....36 B5
Firmins Ct RCOLW CO6.....16 A5

Firs Cha K/T/MI CO5.....63 F5
Firs Hamlet K/T/MI CO5.....9 E5
Firs Rd K/T/MI CO5.....59 F5
 K/T/MI CO5.....9 E5
First Av COS CO15.....64 A2
 FOS CO13.....55 F1
 HAR CO12.....11 F5
Firstore Dr COLN CO4.....35 G1
Fir Tree Cl COLN CO4.....27 E3
Firwood's Rd HSTD CO9.....13 E3
Fisin Wk COLW CO3.....33 G3
Fitzgerald Cl MGTR CO11.....8 C5
Fitzgilbert Rd COLS CO2.....35 G2
Fitzwalter Rd COLW CO3.....35 G2
Fitzwilliam Rd COLW CO3.....35 G2
Five Acres WOTN CO14.....42 B3
Fivefields Cl COS CO15.....59 F4
Flagstaff Rd COLS CO2.....35 G2
Flail Cl RCOLE CO7.....50 B2
Flanders Rd COLS CO2.....35 F3
Flatford Dr RCOS CO16.....58 C3
Fleetwood Av COS CO15.....59 F4
Fleetwood Cl COS CO15.....59 F4
Flemish Ct COL CO1.....3 F5
Flixton Cl RCOS CO16.....58 C3
Florence Rd WOTN CO14.....42 D5
Flowers Wy COS CO15.....59 F4
Folkards La RCOLE CO7.....20 B3
The Folly COS CO15.....59 H2
 RCOLE CO7.....20 B3
Ford La COLN CO4.....18 C1
 RCOLE CO7.....18 C1
Ford Rd COS CO15.....59 F5
Fords La COLN CO4.....18 C1
Ford St RCOLW CO6.....14 B5
Fordstreet Hl RCOLW CO6.....14 B5
Fordwich Rd RCOLE CO7.....56 D4
Foresight Rd COLS CO2.....48 D1
Foresters Ct RCOLE CO7 *.....57 E3
Forest Park Av COS CO15.....59 G3
Forest Rd COLN CO4.....27 E3
Forge St RCOLE CO7.....50 B2
Fossetts La RCOLW CO6.....15 H1
Foster Rd HAR CO12.....10 C4
Foundry La RCOLW CO6.....16 A4
Fountain La RCOLW CO6.....31 H4
Fourth Av COS CO15.....64 A2
 FOS CO13.....55 E1
 HSTD CO9.....13 C3
Foxendale Folly COLW CO3 *.....34 A2
Foxes La RCOLW CO6.....32 B5
Foxglove Cl COS CO15.....59 F5
Foxglove Wk COLN CO4.....23 H5
Frances Cl RCOLE CO7.....57 E3
Francis Cl K/T/MI CO5.....63 E3
Francis St RCOLE CO7.....50 B1
Francis Wy COLN CO4.....33 H3
Frank Clater Cl COLN CO4.....18 C5
Frating Rd RCOLE CO7.....39 E3
Freeland Rd COLS CO2.....35 F2
Freelands RCOLE CO7.....57 E3
Fremantle Rd COLS CO2.....35 F3
Frensham Cl COLW CO3.....23 G5
Frere Wy K/T/MI CO5.....67 F3
Freshfields Rd HAR CO12.....10 D5
Freshwater La COS CO15.....59 H5
Friars Cl COLN CO4.....26 A2
 RCOS CO16.....58 C3
Friars Ct COLS CO2 *.....2 C7
Friday Wood Gn COLS CO2.....48 B5
Frietuna Rd FOS CO13.....42 D5
Frinton Rd COS CO15.....60 C3
 FOS CO13.....55 G1
Frog Hall Cl K/T/MI CO5.....67 H5
Fronk's Av HAR CO12.....11 E5
Fronk's Rd HAR CO12.....11 E5
Fryatt Av HAR CO12.....11 F4
Fuchsia Wy RCOS CO16.....27 E5
Fuller's Cl K/T/MI CO5.....63 E3
Fullers Rd COLS CO2.....35 F3
Fulmar Cl COLN CO4.....27 G4
Furneaux La K/T/MI CO5.....52 C4
Furrow Cl COLW CO3 *.....34 A2
Furze Crs RCOLE CO7.....39 E1

G

The Gables HAR CO12 *.....11 E5
Gadwall Reach K/T/MI CO5.....52 D4
Gager Dr K/T/MI CO5.....52 C4
Gainsborough Cl K/T/MI CO5.....67 F3
 RCOS CO16.....58 C3
Gainsborough Dr MGTR CO11.....8 C4
Gainsborough Rd COLW CO3.....35 G1
Gainsford Av COS CO15.....60 D4
The Gap COS CO15.....55 F1
Garden Ct FOS CO13 *.....55 E1
Garden Dr COLW CO3.....35 G1
Gardeners Rd HSTD CO9.....12 D3
Garden Farm K/T/MI CO5.....52 C4
Gardenia Pl RCOS CO16.....27 E5
Gardenia Wk COLN CO4.....23 H5
Garden Rd COS CO15.....60 D4
 WOTN CO14.....42 D5
Garden Yd HSTD CO9 *.....12 D3
Garland Rd HAR CO12.....10 D4
Garrod Ct COLS CO2.....35 F3
Garthwood Cl RCOLW CO6.....16 A5
Gascoigne Rd COLW CO3.....34 B1
Gatefield Cl WOTN CO14.....42 B3
Gavin Wy COLN CO4.....18 C5
Gazelle Ct COLN CO4.....18 C5
Gentian Ct COLN CO4.....27 E5
Geoff Seaden Cl COL CO1.....3 K7
George Av RCOLE CO7.....49 E1
George Cl COS CO15.....59 F4
George Cut RCOLE CO7.....50 B2
George St COL CO1.....3 F5
 HAR CO12.....11 G2
George Williams Wy COL CO1.....2 D6

Ley Fld *RCOLW* C06 ....31 H4
Leys Rd *RCOLE* C07 ....38 B4
Leyton Ct *COS* C015 ....59 F1
Lichfield Cl *COL* C01 ....3 F4
Lilac Ct *RCOLE* C07 ....37 H5
Lilian Impey Dr *COLN* C04 ....18 C4
Lilley's La *RCOLE* C07 ....21 H5
Lime Av *COLN* C04 ....27 E4
  HAR C012 ....11 E4
Lime Cl *COS* C015 ....64 C1
The Limes *COS* C015 * 5 G3
  RCOLE C07 * 21 E2
Lime St *RCOLE* C07 ....57 E5
Lincoln Wy *COL* C01 ....3 F5
Linden Cl *COLN* C04 ....27 F3
Linden Dr *COS* C015 ....59 E3
The Lindens *COLW* C03 * 25 E5
Link Cl *COLW* C04 ....17 H5
Little Rd *COS* C015 ....12 C4
  HSTD C09 ....12 C4
  RCOLE C07 ....57 F4
Linley Gdns *COS* C015 ....4 A5
Linnets *COS* C015 ....59 F3
Linstead Cl *RCOLE* C07 ....58 A5
Lion Wk *COL* C01 * 2 C6
Lisle Rd *COS* C02 ....36 B2
Litchfield Cl *COS* C015 ....59 E4
Litchfield Rd *COS* C015 ....59 E4
Little Bakers *WOTN* C014 ....42 C4
Little Bromley Rd *RCOLE* C07 ...21 F2
Littlebury Gdns *COS* C02 ....36 D3
Little Clacton Rd *RCOLE* C016 ...58 B2
Littlecotes *COLN* C04 ....17 G5
Littlefield Rd *COLS* C02 ....47 F1
Little Harrods *WOTN* C014 ....42 C4
Little Stone Ct *COS* C015 ....64 C4
Little Wd *FOS* C015 ....42 A5
Lockhart Av *COLW* C03 ....25 F5
Lock Rd *HSTD* C09 ....12 D4
Lodge Cl *COS* C015 ....5 G4
Lodge Ct *RCOLW* C06 ....16 C5
Lodge La *COLN* C04 ....19 E1
  RCOLE C07 ....20 B3
  RCOLE C07 ....56 C5
Lodge Rd *RCOLE* C07 ....56 D2
London Rd *COLW* C03 ....33 G1
  COS C015 ....59 E4
  K/T/MI C05 ....53 E2
  RCOLW C06 ....16 B1
  RCOLW C06 ....31 H4
  RCOLW C06 ....32 B3
  RCOS C016 ....58 D1
Longacre *COS* C02 ....25 G2
Longcroft Rd *COLN* C04 ....3 K4
Longdyve *COLS* C02 * 35 G3
Long La *COS* C015 ....24 C3
Long Mdw *HAR* C012 ....10 C5
Longridge *COLN* C04 ....18 B4
Longstraw Cl *COLW* C03 ....34 A1
Long Wyre St *COL* C01 ....2 D6
Lord Holland Rd *COLS* C02 ...36 A4
Lordswood Rd *COLS* C02 ....35 F5
Lorkin Wy *RCOLW* C06 ....16 C5
Love La *RCOLE* C07 ....56 D2
Love Wy *RCOS* C016 ....58 C3
Lowe Cha *WOTN* C014 ....42 D2
Lower Marine Pde *HAR* C012 ...11 F5
Lower Park Rd *RCOLE* C07 ...56 D4
Lower Rd *COLS* C02 ....45 F5
Lucas Av *RCOLW* C06 ....14 C4
Lucas Rd *COLS* C02 ....36 A1
Lucerne Rd *RCOLE* C07 ....39 F1
Lucius Crs *COLN* C04 ....18 C3
Lucy Cl *COLW* C03 ....33 H1
Lucy La North *COLW* C03 ....23 H5
Lucy La South *COLW* C03 ....23 H5
Luff Wy *WOTN* C014 ....42 B4
Lufkin Rd *COLN* C04 ....26 A1
Lugar Cl *COLN* C04 ....37 F1
Lulworth Cl *COS* C015 ....64 C4
Lumber Leys *WOTN* C014 ....42 C4
Lupin Wy *COS* C02 ....35 H2
Lushington Av *FOS* C013 ....41 H5
Lushington Rd *MGTR* C011 ....8 D5
Luther Dr *K/T/MI* C05 ....63 F3
Lydgate Cl *WOTN* C014 ....42 B5
Lymington Av *COS* C015 ....59 F1
Lyndhurst Rd *COS* C015 ....60 A5
Lynne Cl *FOS* C015 ....41 H5
Lynton Cl *HAR* C012 ....11 E3
Lyon Cl *COS* C015 ....5 H1

M

Mabbitt Wy *COLN* C04 ....18 C4
Macbeth Cl *COLS* C02 ....27 G5
Mackay Ct *COLS* C02 ....48 C1
Madeira Rd *COS* C015 ....60 B5
Magazine Farm Wy *COLW* C03 ...34 D2
Magdalen Cl *COS* C015 ....5 G4
Magdalen Gn *COL* C01 * 3 G7
Magdalen Rd *COS* C015 ....4 C1
Magdalen St *COL* C01 ....3 G7
Magnolia Dr *COLN* C04 ....27 G4
Magnus Dr *COLN* C04 ....18 C3
Maidenburgh St *COL* C01 ....2 D5
Main Rd *FOS* C013 ....54 A3
  HAR C012 ....10 D5
  HAR C012 ....11 E4
Makins Rd *HAR* C012 ....10 C2
Maldon Rd *COLS* C02 ....45 F4
  COLW C03 ....35 F2
  K/T/MI C05 ....52 C5
Maldon Road Rbt *COLS* C02 ...2 A7
Maldon Wy *RCOS* C016 ....58 B1
Mallard Cl *COLS* C02 ....46 D5
  K/T/MI C05 ....52 C3
Mallows Fld *HSTD* C09 ....12 D3
Malthouse Rd *MGTR* C011 ....9 E5
Malting Green Rd *COLS* C02 ...46 C5

Malting La *FOS* C013 ....41 G2
Malting Rd *COLS* C02 ....47 F1
Maltings Pk *RCOLW* C06 * 16 C5
Maltings Rd *RCOLE* C07 ....56 D2
Malting Yd *RCOLE* C07 ....50 A2
Maltings Park Rd *RCOLW* C06 ...16 C5
Malvern Wy *RCOLW* C06 ....17 E2
Manchester Rd *COS* C015 ....60 C5
Mandeville Rd *RCOLW* C06 ....31 F4
Mandeville Wy *FOS* C013 ....42 B4
Manningtree Rd *RCOLE* C07 ...6 D3
Manor Cl *RCOLW* C06 ....17 F2
Manor Gdns *COLW* C03 * 25 G5
Manor House Wy *RCOLE* C07 ...56 D3
Manor La *HAR* C012 ....11 G4
Manor Rd *COLW* C03 ....2 A6
  FOS C013 ....54 A3
  HAR C012 ....10 D4
  RCOLE C07 ....50 B1
  RCOS C016 ....16 B4
Manor Wy *COS* C015 ....64 B1
  HAR C012 ....11 E4
  HSTD C09 ....13 F2
Maple Cl *DOS* C013 ....41 H5
Maple Leaf *K/T/MI* C05 ....62 D1
Maple Wy *COLS* C02 ....48 B3
Marasca End *COLS* C02 ....48 B3
Maraschino Crs *COLS* C02 ....48 B3
Marcus Ct *COLN* C04 ....18 C3
Marennes Crs *RCOLE* C07 ....56 D3
Mareth Rd *COLS* C02 ....35 F5
Margaret Ct *RCOLE* C07 ....57 E4
Margaret Rd *COL* C01 ....2 B5
Maria St *HAR* C012 ....11 G2
Marigold Av *RCOS* C016 ....58 C4
Marigold Cl *COLN* C04 ....27 F4
Marina Gdns *COS* C015 ....60 A4
Marina Ms *WOTN* C014 ....43 E3
Marine Ct *FOS* C013 * 55 F2
Marine Pde *HAR* C012 ....11 G4
Marine Pde East *COS* C015 ....4 E5
Marine Pde West *COS* C015 ...4 C7
Marion Av *RCOS* C016 ....59 E3
Market Cl *COL* C01 * 2 C5
Market St *HAR* C012 * 11 H1
Marlborough Ct *COS* C015 ....64 C1
Marlowe Rd *COS* C015 ....64 A3
Marlowe Wy *COLW* C03 ....24 C5
Marne Rd *COLS* C02 ....35 H3
Marney Wy *FOS* C015 ....42 D5
Marram Cl *COLW* C03 ....33 G1
Marshall Cl *K/T/MI* C05 ....52 D2
Marsh Crs *K/T/MI* C05 ....49 G2
Marsh Wy *COLS* C02 ....56 D4
Martello Rd *WOTN* C014 ....43 E3
Martin End *COS* C02 ....48 C3
Martinsdale *COS* C015 ....59 F5
Martin's Rd *HSTD* C09 * 12 D3
Maryborough Gv *COLS* C02 ...36 C5
Mary Warner Rd *RCOLE* C07 ...20 D2
Mascot Sq *COLN* C04 ....37 E2
Mascot Cl *COS* C02 ....36 B5
Mason Cl *COL* C01 ....35 E4
Mason Rd *COL* C01 ....2 C2
  RCOS C016 ....64 B1
Mathews Cl *HSTD* C09 ....13 F1
Maudlyn Rd *COLN* C04 ....36 D1
Maulsham Dr *COLN* C04 ....18 B3
Mayberry Wy *COLS* C02 ....36 B4
Maybury Cl *RCOLW* C06 ....31 G4
Mayda Ct *HSTD* C09 ....12 C3
Mayfair Ct *COS* C02 * 36 D3
Mayfield Cl *COLN* C04 ....3 J1
Mayflower Av *HAR* C012 ....11 F5
Mayflower Cl *COLW* C03 * 34 A1
Mayflower Dr *WOTN* C014 ....36 D5
Maypole Green Rd *COLS* C02 ...47 F1
Maypole Rd *COLS* C02 ....62 D2
May's La *RCOLE* C07 ....6 B5
Meadow Cl *COS* C015 ....59 H2
  HSTD C09 ....13 E4
Meadowcroft Wy *FOS* C013 ...42 B4
Meadow Grass Cl *COLW* C03 ...33 C1
Meadow La *K/T/MI* C05 ....66 D5
Meadow Rd *COLS* C02 ....47 C1
Meadows Cl *RCOLE* C07 ....39 E1
Meadow Vw *K/T/MI* C05 ....63 E3
Meadow View Cl *COLN* C04 ...34 B2
Meadow View Pk *RCOS* C016 * ...13 E3
Mede Wy *COLW* C03 ....38 B4
Medusa Ct *HAR* C012 ....11 E5
The Meers *FOS* C015 ....42 A5
Melbourne Cha *COLS* C02 ....48 C1
Melbourne Rd *COS* C015 ....4 A3
Mellor Cha *COLW* C03 ....24 B5
Melrose Gdns *COS* C015 ....60 A4
Melrose Rd *K/T/MI* C05 ....66 C4
Melton Ct *RCOS* C016 ....58 A5
Mendlesham Rd *RCOS* C016 ...38 B5
Menin Rd *COLS* C02 ....55 C5
Mercers Wy *COL* C01 ....2 B3
Meredith Rd *COS* C015 ....4 C3
Meriden End *COLN* C04 ....59 G4
Merlin End *COLN* C04 ....27 G3
Merriam Cl *MGTR* C011 ....8 B3
Merrilees Crs *COS* C015 ....60 B3
Merrymount Gdns *COS* C015 ...59 H4
Mersea Av *K/T/MI* C05 ....66 C4
Mersea Rd *COLS* C02 ....48 B1
Merstham Dr *RCOS* C016 ....58 C3
Merton Ct *COLS* C02 * 48 B3
Messines Rd *COLS* C02 ....35 B5
Meyrick Crs *COLS* C02 ....36 A2
Middleborough *COL* C01 ....2 B4
Middlefield *HSTD* C09 ....13 E3
Middle Mi *COL* C01 ....2 C4
Middleton Cl *RCOS* C016 ....58 A3
Middlewick Cl *COLS* C02 ....48 B1
Midland Cl *COLS* C02 ....36 A3
Midway Rd *COLS* C02 ....35 F5
Mile End Rd *COLS* C02 ....25 H2
Miles Cl *COLW* C03 ....33 H1
Milford Cl *RCOLE* C07 ....50 B1
Military Rd *COL* C01 ....36 B2

Mill Cha *HSTD* C09 ....12 D2
Mill Cl *K/T/MI* C05 ....62 D2
Miller's Barn Rd *COS* C015 ...64 A3
Millers Cl *COLW* C03 ....33 H1
  RCOLW C06 ....17 E2
Millers La *COLW* C03 ....34 A1
Millers Md *K/T/MI* C05 ....53 E2
Millfields *COLS* C02 * 47 F5
Mill Hi *MGTR* C011 ....7 G5
Mill La *COLS* C02 ....11 G4
  HAR C012 ....11 G4
  K/T/MI C05 ....30 A5
  MGTR C011 ....9 E5
  RCOLE C07 ....21 G5
  RCOLE C07 ....43 E2
  WOTN C014 ....43 E2
Mill Rd *COLN* C04 ....17 H5
  RCOLW C06 ....66 D2
  RCOS C016 ....14 C5
  RCOS C016 ....32 B5
Mill St *COL* C01 ....36 B1
  RCOLE C07 ....57 F4
Mill Wk *K/T/MI* C05 ....53 E4
Millwrights *K/T/MI* C05 ....64 C2
Milton Cl *COLW* C03 ....34 C1
Milton Rd *HAR* C012 ....11 G3
Minerva Cl *HAR* C012 ....10 C5
Minsmere Dr *RCOS* C016 ....58 C3
Miranda Wk *COL* C01 ....27 F5
Mitchell Av *HSTD* C09 ....12 D3
Moat Flds *RCOLW* C06 ....14 C4
Moat Rd *RCOLW* C04 ....14 C4
Modien Rd *WOTN* C014 ....42 C4
Monklands Ct *HSTD* C09 ....12 C3
Monk's La *RCOLE* C07 ....6 A5
Monkwick Av *COLS* C02 ....35 G5
Mons Rd *COLS* C02 ....35 G3
Montfitchet Cl *COLW* C03 ....34 A1
Montgomery Cl *COLS* C02 ....36 C3
Moorhouse Gn *RCOLE* C07 ...20 D1
Moorside *COL* C01 ....3 H6
Morant Rd *COL* C01 ....3 G6
Morello Ct *COLS* C02 ....48 B3
Morley Rd *HSTD* C09 ....13 E2
  K/T/MI C05 ....63 E4
Morrow La *RCOLE* C07 ....21 F3
Morses La *RCOLE* C07 ....57 E2
Morten Rd *COL* C01 ....3 H5
Morton Wy *HSTD* C09 ....13 F1
Mossfield Ct *COLW* C03 ....35 F1
Moss Rd *COLW* C03 ....34 B3
Moss Wy *RCOLW* C06 ....24 B1
Mott's La *COLS* C02 ....31 E3
Mountain Ash Cl *COLN* C04 ...26 D2
Mountbatten Dr *COLS* C02 ...36 C4
Mount Wy *HSTD* C09 ....12 C3
Mount Pleasant *HSTD* C09 ...12 D3
Mount Pleasant Ms
  HSTD C09 * 12 D3
Mount Ri *HSTD* C09 ....12 D3
The Mount *COLW* C03 ....34 C1
Mountview Rd *COS* C015 ....59 G4
Moy Rd *COLS* C02 ....35 H3
Mulberry Av *COLS* C02 ....36 B3
Mulberry Wk *K/T/MI* C05 * 63 E3
Mulberry Rd *RCOLW* C06 ....16 A5
Mumford Cl *RCOLW* C06 ....14 B3
Mumford Rd *RCOLW* C04 ....26 A1
Mumfords La *FOS* C015 ....41 E4
Munnings Dr *RCOS* C016 ....58 D3
Munnings Rd *COLN* C04 ....34 D2
Munnings Wy *MGTR* C011 ....8 C4
Muscade Cl *K/T/MI* C05 ....63 E2
Museum St *COL* C01 ....2 D6
Musk Cl *COLW* C04 ....24 A5
Muswell Wk *RCOS* C016 ....58 D3
Mychett Cl *COS* C02 ....58 B5
Myland Hall Cha *COLN* C04 ...26 D1
Mynott Ct *K/T/MI* C05 * 63 E4
Myrtle Gv *COL* C01 ....36 C2

N

Nancy Smith Cl *COLS* C02 ....36 A2
Nansen Rd *COS* C015 ....60 B3
Napier Rd *COLS* C02 ....36 A1
Nash Cl *COLW* C03 ....35 E2
  MGTR C011 ....8 C4
Nathan Ct *COLS* C02 ....48 C2
Nayland Dr *RCOS* C016 ....58 B5
Nayland Rd *COLN* C04 ....17 G4
  RCOLW C06 ....16 A3
Naze Park Rd *WOTN* C014 ....43 F1
Neale Rd *HSTD* C09 ....12 D3
Neasden Av *RCOS* C016 ....58 D4
Nelson Rd *COLW* C03 ....34 B5
  COS C015 ....4 C6
  HAR C012 ....11 F5
Nelson St *RCOLE* C07 ....56 D5
Neptune Ct *COL* C01 * 9 E1
Nether Ct *HSTD* C09 ....13 F5
Newbridge Hi *RCOLW* C06 ...24 A2
Newbridge Rd *K/T/MI* C05 ...63 G3
New Captains Rd *K/T/MI* C05 ...66 C4
Newcastle Av *COLW* C03 ....34 B3
New Church Rd *RCOLW* C06 ...16 A5
Newcomen Wy *COLS* C02 ....18 D5
New Cut *COLS* C02 ....46 C5
New Farm Rd *COLS* C02 ....48 C3
Newgate St *WOTN* C014 ....43 E3
Newington Gdns *COS* C015 ...59 F1
New Kiln Rd *COLW* C03 ....35 F5
New La *COLS* C02 ....36 C1
New Park St *COS* C015 ....36 F1
New Pier St *WOTN* C014 ....43 E3
Newport Dr *COS* C015 ....59 C2
Newport Wy *FOS* C015 ....42 C5
New Rd *K/T/MI* C05 ....63 E3
  K/T/MI C05 ....63 E3
  MGTR C011 ....9 G5
  RCOLW C06 ....22 A2
New St *HSTD* C09 ....12 C3

RCOLW C06 ....16 A5
Owls Retreat *COLN* C04 ....9 F5
Oxborrow Cl *FOS* C015 ....
Oxford Ct *COLW* C03 * ....
Oxford Crs *COS* C015 ....
Oxford Rd *COLW* C03 ....
  COS C015 ....
  FOS C015 ....
  HSTD C09 ....
Oxley Parker Dr *COLN* C04 ....
Oxton Cl *K/T/MI* C05 ....
Oyster Tank Rd *RCOLE* C07 ....
Ozier Fld *HSTD* C09 ....

P

Packe Cl *K/T/MI* C05 ....
Paddock Cl *HAR* C012 ....
Paddock Wy *RCOLE* C07 ....
Page Rd *COS* C015 ....
Paget Rd *K/T/MI* C05 ....
  RCOLE C07 * ....
Palfrey Hts *MGTR* C011 ....
Pallister Rd *COS* C015 ....
Pampas Cl *COLN* C04 ....
Pantlings La *K/T/MI* C05 ....
Panton Crs *COLN* C04 ....
Papillon Rd *COLW* C03 ....
The Parade *COS* C02 * ....
  WOTN C014 ....
Park Bvd *COS* C015 ....
Park Dr *HSTD* C09 ....
  RCOLE C07 ....
Parker Wy *HSTD* C09 ....
Parkeston Quay *HAR* C012 ....
Parkeston Rd *HAR* C012 ....
Parkeston Rbt *HAR* C012 ....
Parkfield St *K/T/MI* C05 ....
Park Rd *COLN* C04 ....
  COLW C03 ....
  COS C015 ....
  HAR C012 ....
  RCOLE C07 ....
  RCOLE C07 ....
Parkside Quarter *COL* C01 ....
Park Ter *HAR* C012 * ....
Park Wy *COS* C015 ....
Parkwood Av *RCOLE* C07 ....
Parnell Ct *COLS* C02 ....
Parr Dr *COLW* C03 ....
Parry Dr *RCOS* C016 ....
Parsonage St *HSTD* C09 ....
Parson's Fld *RCOLE* C07 ....
Parson's Heath *COLN* C04 ....
Parson's Hl *COLW* C03 ....
Parsons La *COL* C01 ....
Parsons Yd *MGTR* C011 * ....
Partridge Dr *RCOLW* C06 ....
Paternoster Rw
  WOTN C014 * ....
Pathfields Rd *COS* C015 ....
Patmore Rd *COLN* C04 ....
Patten Cl *RCOLW* C06 ....
Pattern Bush Cl *MGTR* C011 ...
Pattrick's La *HAR* C012 ....
Pauline Cl *COS* C015 ....
Pauls Crs *RCOLE* C07 ....
Paul Spendlove Ct
  COLN C04 * ....
Paxman Av *COLS* C02 ....
Paxton Rd *COS* C015 ....
Paynters Ter *HSTD* C09 * ....
Peacehaven *FOS* C015 ....
Peace Rd *COLW* C03 ....
Peake Av *FOS* C015 ....
Peakes Cl *K/T/MI* C05 ....
Pearmain Wy *COLW* C015 ....
Peartree Rd *COLW* C03 ....
Pebmarsh Cl *COLS* C02 ....
Pedder's Cl *COS* C02 ....
Peerswood Rd *COLS* C02 ....
Pegasus Wy *COLN* C04 ....
Pelham Cl *HAR* C012 ....
Pelhams La *COL* C01 ....
Pembroke Cl *COLS* C02 ....
Pembroke Gdns *COS* C015 ....
Penfold Rd *COS* C015 ....
Penlan Hall La *RCOLW* C06 ...
Pennsylvania La
  K/T/MI C05 ....
Penrice Cl *COLN* C04 ....
Penzance Ct *COS* C015 ....
Peppercorn Cl *COLN* C04 ....
Pepys St *HAR* C012 ....
Percival Rd *FOS* C015 ....
  WOTN C014 ....
Peregrine Cl *COS* C015 ....
Peregrine Ct *COLN* C04 ....
Perry Rd *K/T/MI* C05 ....
Persardi Ct *COS* C02 ....
Pershore End *COLW* C03 ....
Perth Cl *COS* C02 ....
Pertwee Cl *RCOLE* C07 ....
Pertwees Ct *COS* C01 ....
Peter Bruff Av *RCOS* C016 ....
Peto Av *COLN* C04 ....
Petrolea Cl *COL* C01 ....
Petronius Wy *COLN* C04 ....
Petworth Ct *RCOLE* C07 ....
Pevensey Dr *COS* C015 ....
Pharos La *K/T/MI* C05 ....
Philip Cl *WOTN* C014 ....
Phillip Rd *RCOLE* C07 ....
Pickers Wy *COS* C015 ....
Pier Ap *WOTN* C014 ....
Pier Av *COS* C015 ....
Pierce Gld *K/T/MI* C05 ....
Pier Gap *COS* C015 ....
Pightle Wy *WOTN* C014 ....
Pilborough Wy *COLN* C04 ....
Pine Cl *MGTR* C011 ....
Pinecroft Gdns *COLW* C03 ...

O

Oakapple Cl *COLS* C02 ....47 G1
Oak Av *COS* C015 ....64 A2
Oak Cl *RCOLW* C06 ....24 B1
Oak Holm *COLS* C02 ....36 B4
Oakland Rd *HAR* C012 ....11 F4
Oaklands Av *COLW* C03 ....26 B4
Oakleigh Rd *COS* C015 ....59 F1
Oakley Cl *HSTD* C09 ....12 C4
Oaks Cl *COLW* C03 ....25 C3
Oaks Pl *COLN* C04 ....25 H1
The Oaks *FOS* C015 ....42 B5
Oak Tree Rd *RCOLE* C07 ....51 C2
Oakwood Av *COS* C015 ....67 E3
  K/T/MI C05 ....67 E3
Oakwood Cl *FOS* C015 ....42 A5
Oakwood Dr *K/T/MI* C05 ....67 E3
Oakwood Gdns *K/T/MI* C05 ...67 E3
Oak Yd *HSTD* C09 * 12 C3
Oatfield Cl *COLW* C03 ....34 A1
Oatlands *RCOLE* C07 ....39 E1
Oberon Cl *COLN* C04 ....27 G5
Observer Wy *K/T/MI* C05 ....52 B2
Ockendon Wy *WOTN* C014 ...42 C4
Old Coach Rd *COL* C01 ....3 H5
Old Ferry Rd *RCOLE* C07 ....50 A2
Old Forge Rd *COLS* C02 ....46 C5
Old Heath Rd *COLS* C02 ....36 A3
Old House Rd *RCOLW* C06 ...16 C1
Old Ipswich Rd *RCOLE* C07 ...19 F5
Old Parsonage Wy
  FOS C015 ....55 F1
Old Pier St *WOTN* C014 ....43 E3
Old Rd *COS* C015 ....4 C2
Old Rose Gdns *COLN* C04 * ...17 G5
Old School La *RCOLE* C07 ....39 F1
Old Vicarage Rd *HAR* C012 ...11 F4
Old Wy *FOS* C013 ....55 F2
Olive Gv *COLS* C02 ....35 G5
Olivers Cl *COS* C015 ....59 E4
Olivers Ct *COS* C015 * 59 E5
Olivers La *COLS* C02 ....46 C5
Olivers Rd *COS* C015 ....4 D1
Olley Wk *K/T/MI* C05 ....63 F2
Ongar Cl *RCOS* C016 ....58 B5
Onslow Crs *COLS* C02 ....48 B1
Ophir Rd *RCOLE* C07 ....57 F4
Orchard Av *HSTD* C09 ....12 C5
Orchard Cl *RCOLE* C07 ....39 F1
  RCOLW C06 ....32 C5
  RCOS C016 ....58 C4
Orchard Dr *FOS* C013 ....54 A2
Orchard Gdns *COLN* C04 ....3 K3
Orchard Ldg *K/T/MI* C05 * 63 E4
Orchard Ms *K/T/MI* C05 ....62 D4
Orchard Rd *COL* C01 ....2 C3
  K/T/MI C05 ....52 C3
  RCOLE C07 ....51 D2
Orlando Ct *WOTN* C014 ....43 E3
Ormonde Ct *RCOLW* C06 ....16 C5
Orpen Cl *RCOLW* C06 ....15 C2
Orpen's Hl *COLW* C03 ....45 F4
Orwell Cl *COLN* C04 ....27 F3
Orwell Rd *COS* C015 ....4 E5
  HAR C012 ....11 G3
Orwell Wy *RCOS* C016 ....58 C4
Osborne Ct *COS* C015 ....59 C2
Osborne Rd *K/T/MI* C05 ....66 C4
Osbornes Rd *RCOLE* C07 ....57 E4
Osborne St *COL* C01 ....2 D7
Ospreys *COS* C015 ....59 F3
Othello Cl *COLN* C04 ....27 G4
Ottershaw Wy *RCOS* C016 ...58 B5
Oulton Cl *HAR* C012 ....10 C4
Outpart Eastward
  HAR C012 * 11 H1
Owen Ward Cl *COLS* C02 ....34 D4

/T/MI CO5 66 C3
l Cl COS CO15 59 E2
13 41 H5
l COL CO1 * 36 B1
COLW CO3 25 E5
ns HSTD CO9 12 C2
COLW CO6 16 B5
/MI CO5 62 D2
m Cl RCOLE CO7 19 E3
w Cl COS CO15 64 B2
Vy RCOLE CO7 56 C3
Pl MGTR CO11 * 9 H5
COLW CO3 34 D2
ans Headland
CO3 34 A2
FOS CO13 42 A5
COLW CO3 34 D3
s Rd RCOLW CO6 14 D3
Rd COS CO15 64 D4
La FOS CO13 55 F1
k RCOS CO16 58 C4
Wy RCOS CO16 58 B5
COLW CO3 34 D3
Rd RCOLW CO6 22 B1
Rd COLN CO4 27 E3
ne Rd COLS CO2 36 A3
COLW CO3 2 A6
COS CO15 64 A2
COS CO15 64 B2
O9 13 E4
RCOLE CO7 51 G3
y FOS CO13 41 H5
ns COLS CO2 36 D4
OS CO13 40 C5
rook Wk COLN CO4 26 D2
l COLW CO3 23 E2
a COLW CO3 23 E2
y RCOS CO16 58 B5
Av HAR CO12 11 F4
Crs HAR CO12 * 11 F4
Rd COL CO1 2 D7
OL CO1 36 C1
Cl MGTR CO11 9 H5
o Rd WOTN CO14 43 E3
uth Rd COS CO15 64 C4
Ct HSTD CO9 13 E1
t COLN CO4 18 A4
rm Dr HAR CO12 10 C4
ld Cl RCOLE CO7 * 51 G3
Crs COLS CO2 36 A3
Pl FOS CO13 42 A4
t Rd COLW CO3 34 B2
Rd COS CO15 60 B4
Rd HSTD CO9 13 E2
e Rd COLW CO3 34 D3
La K/T/MI CO5 62 D2
Rd COS CO15 60 C3
Wk COLN CO4 27 F4
bert Rd K/T/MI CO5 66 D4
arles Cl COS CO15 64 C3
arles Rd COLS CO2 48 A1
a RCOLE CO7 6 C2
ilip Av COS CO15 64 C3
ilip Rd COLS CO2 48 A1
Esp WOTN CO14 43 F3
d COS CO15 60 B4
O12 11 E4
Anne Cl COS CO15 64 C3
St HAR CO12 10 C2
n Ms COLN CO4 18 C5
STD CO9 12 C4
COLN CO4 25 G2
COS CO15 4 C3
I8 62 A5
COL CO1 2 E6
k COL CO1 2 D6
Wy RCOLW CO6 31 F4
de HAR CO12 11 F5
de Wy RCOLE CO7 56 C5
Cl COLN CO4 27 G5
e Cl COLW CO3 23 H5
ce Pl COL CO1 3 G7
t COLS CO2 48 B3
ale COS CO15 59 F4
d Cl WOTN CO14 42 C3
COLN CO4 37 F1
y RCOS CO16 58 B3
y COLN CO4 18 C4
Cl K/T/MI CO5 50 B4
CO7 56 D3
FOS CO13 41 G3

Q

FOS CO13 41 H2
MGTR CO11 9 E5
CO7 50 A3
y HAR CO12 11 G1
CO7 50 A3
nne Dr K/T/MI CO5 67 E4
nne Gdns K/T/MI CO5 67 E4
nne Rd K/T/MI CO5 67 E4
ry Cl K/T/MI CO5 67 E4
lizabeth Av
O15 64 C3
lizabeth Wy COLS CO2 48 B1
ary Av COLS CO2 36 B3
ury Av RCOLW CO6 32 D2
and Dr COLS CO2 48 B1
Rd COLW CO3 35 F1
O15 64 C3
O13 55 F2
O12 10 D5
CO7 50 A2
V CO6 24 A1
COL CO1 2 D6
CO7 57 E4
ay COS CO15 60 B4
I CO5 62 D2
CO11 8 D5
Wy FOS CO13 42 C5
Cl COS CO15 60 D3

R

Raeburn Cl FOS CO13 42 B4
Raglan Ms COS CO15 64 C1
Raglan Rd FOS CO13 55 F1
Railway Cottages COS CO15 4 E2
Railway St MGTR CO11 9 E5
Railway Ter MGTR CO11 * 9 E5
Rainbow Rd K/T/MI CO5 67 E4
Rainham Wy FOS CO13 42 D5
Rainsborowe Rd COLS CO2 35 F3
Rambler Cl COLW CO3 24 A5
Ramparts Cl RCOLW CO6 17 E2
Ramparts Ct COLN CO4 * 25 E2
Ramplings Av COS CO15 59 E4
Ramsden Cl COS CO15 59 G4
Ramsey Rd HAR CO12 10 A5
HSTD CO9 12 C4
Ranger Wk COLS CO2 36 C4
Rangoon Cl COLS CO2 47 E1
Ransom Rd K/T/MI CO5 62 D3
Ratcliffe Ct K/T/MI CO5 52 B4
Ratcliffe Rd COLW CO3 34 B2
Ravens Av HSTD CO9 13 E4
Ravensdale COS CO15 59 F3
Raven Wy COLN CO4 17 H5
Rawden Cl HAR CO12 11 E3
Rawlings Crs COLN CO4 18 C4
Rawstorn Rd COLW CO3 2 A6
Ray Av HAR CO12 10 D3
Raycliff Av RCOS CO16 59 E2
Ray La HAR CO12 10 B2
Rayleigh Cl COLN CO4 3 G2
The Rayleighs COLW CO3 * 35 F2
Rayner Rd COLS CO2 35 E3
Rayner Wy HSTD CO9 12 D3
Reaper Rd COLW CO3 34 D3
Rebow Rd HAR CO12 10 D5
RCOLE CO7 50 A2
Rebow St COL CO1 36 C1
Reckitts Cl COS CO15 5 J1
Recreation Rd COL CO1 36 C2
COS CO15 5 F2
Recreation Wy RCOLE CO7 57 E3
Rectory Cl COLN CO4 25 H2
Rectory Hl RCOLE CO7 50 B1
Rectory Rd FOS CO13 54 A3
K/T/MI CO5 49 F3
K/T/MI CO5 62 D3
RCOLE CO7 38 B5
RCOLW CO6 44 B1
Red Barn Rd RCOLE CO7 57 E2
Redbridge Rd COS CO15 59 F1
Red Lion Yd COL CO1 * 2 C6
Redmill COLW CO3 34 D4
Redrose Wk RCOS CO16 58 C5
Redwood Cl COLN CO4 27 F4
Reed Cl RCOS CO16 58 C4
Reed Hall Av COLS CO2 35 G4
Refinery Rd HAR CO12 10 B2
Reform Ter MGTR CO11 * 9 E5
Regency Ct COLS CO2 * 36 D3
Regency Gn COLW CO3 34 C3
Regency Ldg COS CO15 * 59 E4
Regent Cl RCOLE CO7 57 E2
Regent Rd RCOLE CO7 57 E3
Regents Cl COLN CO4 18 D4
Regent St K/T/MI CO5 49 G2
MGTR CO11 9 E5
Reigate Av RCOS CO16 58 D3
Rembrandt Wy COLW CO3 35 E2
The Retreat RCOLW CO6 24 B1
Reymead Cl K/T/MI CO5 66 D3
Reynards Cl FOS CO13 41 H5
Reynards Copse COLN CO4 26 B1
Reynolds Av COLW CO3 35 E2
Richard Av RCOLE CO7 38 B4
RCOLE CO7 57 E4
Richardson Wk COLW CO3 34 C2
Richards Wk RCOS CO16 59 E3
Richmond Crs HAR CO12 11 E5
Richmond Dr COS CO15 64 A3
Richmond Rd K/T/MI CO5 67 E4
Riddles Dr COLN CO4 26 A2
The Ridge WOTN CO14 42 D3
Ridgeway COLN CO4 18 B5
The Ridgeway HAR CO12 10 D4
Ridgewell Wy COLS CO2 48 A1
Rimini Cl COLS CO2 35 F5
Ripley Cl RCOS CO16 58 B3
Ripple Wy COLN CO4 3 H2
Risby Cl RCOS CO16 58 A5
The Rise RCOLW CO6 23 F4
River Cl HSTD CO9 13 E3
Riverside Av East
MGTR CO11 8 D4
Riverside Av West
MGTR CO11 8 D4
Riverside Wk COL CO1 * 2 B4
Riverside Wy K/T/MI CO5 52 C5
Roach V COLN CO4 27 F3
Roberts Rd COLS CO2 36 A2
Robin Crs COLW CO3 33 G3
Robinsdale COS CO15 59 F3
Robinson Rd RCOLE CO7 57 F3
Rochdale Wy COLN CO4 37 F1
Rochford Wy WOTN CO14 42 C4
Rockingham Cl COLN CO4 27 E1
Roddam Cl COLW CO3 35 F1
Rogation Cl COLW CO3 34 A2
Rokell Wy FOS CO13 42 B5
Rolley La K/T/MI CO5 52 C4
Roman Rd COL CO1 2 E4
Romford Cl COLN CO4 3 H3
Romney Cl FOS CO13 42 A4
RCOLE CO7 56 D1
RCOS CO16 58 D3
Romulus Cl COLN CO4 18 A4
Ronald Rd HSTD CO9 12 D4
The Rookeries RCOLW CO6 32 A3
Rookery La K/T/MI CO5 62 D1
The Rookery MGTR CO11 8 D5
Rookwood Cl RCOS CO16 59 E2
Roosevelt Wy COLS CO2 36 C3
Rosabelle Av RCOLE CO7 50 A1
Rosalind Cl COLN CO4 27 G5
Rose Av COLW CO3 33 H3
Rosebank HAR CO12 10 D4
Rosebank Rd K/T/MI CO5 66 B4
Rosebery Av COL CO1 3 F6
Rose Ct COLS CO2 * 48 C2
Rose Crs COLN CO4 25 G2
Rosecroft Cl COS CO15 59 E3
Rose La RCOLE CO7 50 A3
Rosemary Cl K/T/MI CO5 62 D3
Rosemary Crs COS CO15 5 F5
K/T/MI CO5 62 D3
Rosemary La HSTD CO9 12 D2
Rosemary Rd COS CO15 4 E4
Rosemary Rd West COS CO15 4 C4
Rosemary Wy COS CO15 64 A5
Rosery Ms FOS CO13 54 A2
Rose Vls MGTR CO11 * 9 E1
Rosewood Cl COLN CO4 18 B5
Rose Yd HSTD CO9 * 13 E2
Rossendale Cl COLN CO4 26 D1
Rossetta Cl RCOLE CO7 38 A5
Roundacre HSTD CO9 12 D4
Round Cl COLW CO3 25 E5
Rowallan Cl COLW CO3 34 D4
Rowan Cl COLW CO3 34 A3
COS CO15 64 C1
HAR CO12 11 E4
Rowan Pl COL CO1 2 B2
Rowhedge Rd COLS CO2 37 E5
Rowlands Cl HAR CO12 * 10 B5
Rowland's Yd HAR CO12 10 B5
Rowland Vls MGTR CO11 * 8 B2
Rowley Cl MGTR CO11 9 E1
Royal Ct COLN CO4 27 F3
Roydon Wy FOS CO13 42 B5
Ruaton Dr RCOS CO16 58 C5
Rudkin Rd COLN CO4 18 A4
Rudsdale Wy COLW CO3 34 C2
Rugosa Cl COLW CO3 23 H5
Rush Green Rd RCOS CO16 64 B1
Rushmere Cl K/T/MI CO5 66 D4
Ruskin Cl FOS CO13 42 A4
Russell Rd COS CO15 5 H2
Russell's Rd HSTD CO9 12 B4
Rutland Av COLS CO2 35 E4
Ryde Av COS CO15 59 G2
Rye Cl COLW CO3 34 A2
RCOLE CO7 56 D1
Ryegate Rd COL CO1 2 D4
Rye Hills HSTD CO9 13 E4
Rye Mill La K/T/MI CO5 52 D2

S

Sackville Wy RCOLW CO6 16 A5
Sadler Cl COL CO1 36 C3
Sadlers Cl FOS CO13 41 G5
Saffron Wy K/T/MI CO5 62 D4
Sage Rd COLS CO2 36 B5
St Alban's Rd COLW CO3 25 G5
COS CO15 5 G2
St Andrew's Av COLN CO4 3 J5
St Andrews Cl RCOLE CO7 51 G3
St Andrews Gdns COLN CO4 3 H4
St Andrews Pl RCOLE CO7 56 D1
St Andrew's Rd COS CO15 4 C2
HSTD CO9 12 D2
St Anne's Rd COLN CO4 3 J3
St Anns Rd COS CO15 59 E5
St Augustine Ms COL CO1 2 E6
St Augustines Ct HAR CO12 * 11 F3
St Austell Rd COLN CO4 27 E1
St Austin's La HAR CO12 11 H1
St Barbara's Rd COLS CO2 35 G3
St Bartholomew Cl COLN CO4 26 D1
St Bernard Rd COLN CO4 27 E2
St Botolph's Church Wk
COL CO1 * 2 D7
St Botolphs Circ COL CO1 2 D7
St Botolph's St COL CO1 2 D6
St Botolph's Ter
WOTN CO14 * 43 E3
St Bride Ct COLN CO4 27 E2
St Catherines Cl COLS CO2 47 G1
St Christopher Rd COLN CO4 27 E2
St Clair Cl COS CO15 59 F1
St Clare Dr COLW CO3 24 D5
St Clare Rd COLW CO3 34 D1
St Clement Rd COLN CO4 27 E2
St Columb Ct COLN CO4 26 D2
St Cyrus Rd COLN CO4 27 E2
St Davids Cl COLN CO4 3 K5
St Dominic Rd COLN CO4 27 E2
St Edmund's Ct COLN CO4 3 J4
St Edmund Wy RCOLE CO7 7 G2
St Faith Rd COLN CO4 27 E2
St Fillan Rd COLN CO4 27 E3
St George's Av HAR CO12 11 F5
St Helena Ms COLW CO3 35 G2
St Helena Rd COLW CO3 35 G2
St Helens Av COS CO15 59 G2
St Helen's Gn HAR CO12 11 H1
St Helen's La COL CO1 2 C5
St Ives Cl RCOS CO16 64 B1
St John Gdns COS CO15 59 E3
St John's Av COL CO1 2 C7
St John's Cl COLN CO4 19 E5
St Johns Gn COLS CO2 2 C7
St John's Rd COLN CO4 27 E1
COS CO15 59 E4
RCOLE CO7 50 B3
RCOS CO16 58 B4
St John's St COL CO1 2 B7
St Joseph Rd COLN CO4 26 D1
St Jude Gdns COLN CO4 27 E2
St Judes Cl COLN CO4 27 E2
St Julian Gv COL CO1 2 E7
St Lawrence Rd COLN CO4 27 E2
St Leonard's Rd COL CO1 36 D1
St Leonards Ter COL CO1 * 36 D1
St Luke's Cha K/T/MI CO5 63 E4
St Luke's Cl COLN CO4 27 E2
St Mark Dr COLN CO4 27 E2
St Marks Rd COS CO15 59 E5
St Martins Cl COS CO15 4 C1
St Mary's Flds COLW CO3 2 A5
St Mary's Rd COS CO15 4 C1
FOS CO13 55 G1
K/T/MI CO5 52 C4
St Michael's Cha RCOLW CO6 32 C5
St Michaels Ct MGTR CO11 9 E5
St Michaels Rd COLS CO2 47 F1
HAR CO12 11 E5
St Monance Wy COLN CO4 27 E2
St Neots Cl COLN CO4 27 E2
St Nicholas Rbt HAR CO12 10 D3
St Nicholas St COL CO1 2 D6
St Osyth Rd COS CO15 64 C1
RCOS CO16 58 B1
St Paul's Rd COL CO1 2 A3
COS CO15 5 G3
St Peters Ct COL CO1 * 2 B4
St Peter's Rd K/T/MI CO5 66 C4
St Peter's St COL CO1 2 B4
St Runwald St COL CO1 2 C5
St Saviour Cl COLN CO4 27 E2
St Thomas Cl COLN CO4 27 F2
St Vincent Rd COS CO15 4 B7
Sainty Cl RCOLE CO7 * 50 B2
Salary Cl COLN CO4 27 F3
Salerno Crs COLS CO2 35 F5
Salisbury Av COLW CO3 35 G1
Salisbury Rd COS CO15 60 B4
Salmon Cl COLW CO3 34 C3
Salmon's La RCOLW CO6 30 B3
Salvia Cl RCOS CO16 58 C5
Samsons Cl RCOLE CO7 56 D2
Samson's Rd RCOLE CO7 56 D1
Sanders Dr COLW CO3 25 E5
Sanderson Ms COL CO1 * 2 C5
K/T/MI CO5 49 G2
Sandford Cl RCOLE CO7 50 B2
Sandmartin Crs COLW CO3 33 H3
Sandon Cl RCOLW CO6 17 F2
Sandown Cl COS CO15 59 G1
Sandpiper Cl COLN CO4 27 H5
Sandringham Dr COLS CO2 36 B3
Sandwich Rd COS CO15 64 C4
RCOLE CO7 57 E2
Saran Ct RCOLE CO7 37 H5
Sargeant Cl COLS CO2 36 C4
Sarre Wy RCOLE CO7 56 D2
Saville St WOTN CO14 43 E2
Savill Rd COLS CO2 36 D5
Saxmundham Wy RCOS CO16 64 A1
Saxon Cl COLW CO3 34 C3
HSTD CO9 13 E2
Saxon Wy COS CO15 60 D3
Scarfe Wy COLN CO4 37 F1
Scarletts Rd COL CO1 36 D2
School Cha HSTD CO9 12 D4
School La MGTR CO11 9 G5
RCOLE CO7 6 C2
RCOLW CO6 16 B5
School Rd COLS CO2 36 B5
FOS CO13 55 E1
RCOLE CO7 39 F2
RCOLW CO6 32 C3
Scott Dr COLW CO3 34 C1
Scythe Wy COLW CO3 34 C3
Sea Cornflower Wy
COS CO15 64 A5
Seafield Rd HAR CO12 11 E5
Seafields Gdns COS CO15 60 A4
Seafields Rd COS CO15 60 A4
Sea Flowers Wy COS CO15 64 A5
Sea Glebe Wy COS CO15 64 A5
Sea King Crs COLN CO4 18 C5
Sea Lavender Wy COS CO15 64 A5
Searle Wy COLW CO3 23 G3
Sea Rosemary Wy COS CO15 64 A5
Sea Thistle Wy COS CO15 64 A5
Seaview Av K/T/MI CO5 67 F3
Seaview Gdns RCOLE CO7 57 E3
Seaview Hts WOTN CO14 43 E4
Seaview Rd RCOLE CO7 57 E3
Sebastian Cl COLN CO4 27 F5
Second Av COS CO15 5 K1
FOS CO13 55 E2
HAR CO12 11 F4
HSTD CO9 13 G3
The Seedfield K/T/MI CO5 66 C4
Selby Cl COLS CO2 47 G1
Seldon Rd K/T/MI CO5 63 E3
Selsey Av COS CO15 64 C4
Serpentine Wk COL CO1 2 B3
Severalls La COLN CO4 18 B2
Severn Rd COS CO15 59 F4
Sexton Cl COLS CO2 48 C2
Shaftesbury Av HAR CO12 11 E3
Shakespeare Rd COLW CO3 34 C1
Shanklin Cl COS CO15 59 G1
Shaw Cl FOS CO13 42 B4
Shears Crs K/T/MI CO5 67 E5
Sheepen Pl COLW CO3 2 A4
Sheepen Rd COLW CO3 25 G4
Sheering Wk COLS CO2 36 A5
Sheerwater Ms COLN CO4 27 H4
Shelley Av K/T/MI CO5 63 F3
Shelley Rd COLW CO3 34 C1
RCOS CO16 58 A4
Shepherds Cft COLW CO3 34 A2
Sheppard Cl RCOS CO16 58 D3
Sherbourne Cl FOS CO13 42 B4
Sherbourne Rd COLN CO4 27 G5
Sheriffs Wy RCOS CO16 59 E2
Sherwood Cl COLN CO4 27 E5
Sherwood Dr COS CO15 59 E3
Sherwood Wy K/T/MI CO5 52 D2
Shewell Wk COL CO1 * 2 B6
Shillito Cl COLW CO3 34 C3
The Shipwrights RCOLE CO7 50 A3
Shoebridge's Hl RCOLE CO7 6 B3
Shoreham Rd COS CO15 64 C4
Short Cut Rd COL CO1 2 B5
Shotley Cl RCOS CO16 64 A1
Shrub End Rd COLW CO3 34 D4
Shrubland Ct COS CO15 59 H4
Shrubland Rd COL CO1 * 36 A1
Shums Hl FOS CO13 41 G3
Siena Ms COLS CO2 36 C3
Silcock Cl COLN CO4 26 D2
Silcott St RCOLE CO7 56 D4
Sillett Cl RCOS CO16 58 D3
Silvanus Cl COLW CO3 35 G1
Silverthorne Cl COLS CO2 36 B4
Simons La COL CO1 3 G7
Simpsons La K/T/MI CO5 62 B5
Sinclair Cl COLN CO4 26 A2
Sinnington End COLN CO4 18 D5
Sioux Cl COLN CO4 18 D5
Sir Isaac's Wk COL CO1 2 B6
Siskin Cl COLN CO4 27 G4
Sittang Cl COLS CO2 47 F1
Sitwell Cl MGTR CO11 8 C5
Skelmersdale Rd COS CO15 4 E2
Skelton Cl MGTR CO11 8 D5
Skyrmans Fee FOS CO13 42 A5
Sladburys La COS CO15 60 B2
Slade Rd COS CO15 60 A3
Slate HSTD CO9 13 E3
Slaters Cl FOS CO13 42 B5
Sloe Hl HSTD CO9 12 B2
Slough Farm Rd HSTD CO9 12 C2
Slough La RCOLE CO7 20 D4
RCOLE CO7 38 A1
Smallwood Rd COLS CO2 35 E4
Smeaton Cl COLN CO4 18 D4
Smiths Fld COLS CO2 36 D2
Smythe Cl RCOS CO16 58 C3
Smythies Av COL CO1 3 F6
Snape Cl RCOS CO16 58 A5
Snape Wy FOS CO13 * 42 B4
Sneating Hall La FOS CO13 40 C3
Snowberry Gv COLS CO2 36 B4
Somerset Cl COLS CO2 35 E4
Somers Rd COLW CO3 34 D3
Somme Rd COLS CO2 35 H3
Sorrel Cl COLN CO4 25 F2
Southcliff WOTN CO14 43 E4
Southcliff Pk COS CO15 59 G5
Southcliff Prom WOTN CO14 43 E4
South Cl HSTD CO9 12 D4
Southcroft Cl FOS CO13 41 G5
Southfields RCOLE CO7 6 C3
Southgate Crs K/T/MI CO5 63 F3
Southgreen Gdns RCOS CO16 58 C5
Southland Cl COLN CO4 3 K1
South Strd MGTR CO11 8 D4
South St COLS CO2 35 H1
MGTR CO11 9 E5
South Vw RCOLE CO7 * 6 C3
Southview Dr COS CO15 60 D3
WOTN CO14 43 E4
Southway COL CO1 2 C7
Southwold Wy RCOS CO16 58 A4
Sovereign Crs COLW CO3 * 35 F1
Sparling Cl COLS CO2 35 E5
The Sparlings FOS CO13 41 G3
Spa Rd K/T/MI CO5 53 E2
Sparrows Herne COS CO15 59 F3
Speedwell Rd COLS CO2 37 E5
Spendells Cl WOTN CO14 43 F1
Spindle Wd COLN CO4 18 B5
Spinnaker Cl COS CO15 64 D4
Spinneyfields K/T/MI CO5 63 E2
Sportsway COL CO1 2 D3
Spring Cha RCOLE CO7 38 A5
RCOLE CO7 56 D3
Spring Cl COLN CO4 26 D1
RCOS CO16 58 C4
Springfields RCOLE CO7 57 E4
Spring La COLW CO3 24 D5
RCOLE CO7 38 A5
RCOLW CO6 16 B5
RCOLW CO6 23 F4
Spring Rd K/T/MI CO5 62 D4
RCOLE CO7 57 E3
Spring Sedge Cl COLW CO3 23 H5
Springvalley La RCOLE CO7 28 B1
Spruce Av COLN CO4 27 F4
Spruce Cl K/T/MI CO5 66 C3
Spurgeon St COL CO1 3 K7
The Square COLS CO2 * 35 E4
K/T/MI CO5 * 66 C4
Squirrels Fld COLN CO4 18 A4
Stable Cl COLW CO3 34 A1
K/T/MI CO5 67 F3
Stablefield Rd WOTN CO14 42 C4
Stable Ms K/T/MI CO5 67 F2
Stafford Cl FOS CO13 42 A5
Stalin Rd COLS CO2 36 C3
Stallards Crs FOS CO13 42 A5
Stambridge Rd COS CO15 58 C5
Stammers Rd COLN CO4 18 A5
Standard Rd COL CO1 36 D1
Standley Rd WOTN CO14 43 F2
Stane Fld RCOLW CO6 31 F4
Stanfield Cl COLW CO3 34 B4
Stanley Av RCOLE CO7 57 F3
Stanley Rd COS CO15 64 C2
HSTD CO9 12 C2
RCOLE CO7 50 B1
Stanley Wooster Wy
COLN CO4 27 F5
Stanmore Cl RCOS CO16 58 D4
Stanstead Rd HSTD CO9 13 E4
Stansted Rd COLS CO2 48 B1
Stansted Wy FOS CO13 42 C5
Stanton Hughes Wy MGTR CO11 8 C5
Stanwell St COL CO1 2 C7
Stanwyn Av COS CO15 4 D2
Station Ap FOS CO13 55 F1
Station La HAR CO12 11 F3
Station Rd COS CO15 4 E3
FOS CO13 41 F5
HAR CO12 10 C2
HAR CO12 11 H2
K/T/MI CO5 62 D4

MGTR CO11 .....8 C4
RCOLE CO7 .....20 D5
RCOLE CO7 .....50 A1
RCOLE CO7 .....51 F2
RCOLE CO7 .....56 D4
RCOLW CO6 .....31 H5
Station St WOTN CO14 .....43 E4
Steele Cl RCOLW CO6 * 31 G4
Stephen Cranfield Cl
 K/T/MI CO5 .....49 H3
Stephenson Rd COLN CO4 .....19 E3
 COS CO15 .....59 H1
Sterling Cl COLN CO4 .....34 B2
Stewards Cl FOS CO13 .....42 B4
Stockwell COL CO1 .....2 C5
Stokeash Cl COLN CO4 .....64 A1
The Stokes WOTN CO14 .....42 D2
Stonecrop COLN CO4 .....25 F2
Stoneham Av RCOS CO16 .....58 A5
Stonehill Wy K/T/MI CO5 .....66 B3
Stoneleigh Pk COLW CO3 .....34 C4
Stoney La RCOLE CO7 .....57 F2
Stores Rd HAR CO12 .....62 D2
Stour Rd HAR CO12 .....10 A5
Stour Rd HAR CO12 * 11 G2
Stour St MGTR CO11 * 9 E5
Stour Ter MGTR CO11 * 9 H5
Stourview Av MGTR CO11 .....9 H5
Stour Wk COLN CO4 .....27 F2
Straight Rd COLN CO4 .....17 H1
 COLW CO3 .....34 B1
Stratford Rd COS CO15 .....60 A5
Strawberry La K/T/MI CO5 .....63 F5
The Street FOS CO13 .....41 G2
 K/T/MI CO5 .....53 E1
 RCOLE CO7 .....20 D1
Strood Cl K/T/MI CO5 .....66 C5
Stuart Pawsey Ct RCOLE CO7 * 50 B1
Stubbs Cl FOS CO13 .....42 A4
 MGTR CO11 .....9 E3
Studd's La COLN CO4 .....17 G5
Sudbourne Av RCOS CO16 .....58 A5
Sudbury Rd HSTD CO9 .....13 E1
Suffolk Av K/T/MI CO5 .....67 E5
Suffolk Cl COLN CO4 .....3 H2
 COS CO15 .....60 C2
Suffolk St WOTN CO14 .....43 E5
Sullivan Cl COLN CO4 .....37 F1
Summer Pl WOTN CO14 * 43 F1
Sunbeam Ct K/T/MI CO5 .....49 H2
Sundale Cl COS CO15 .....60 D3
Sundial Pl RCOLE CO7 .....20 C2
Sunningdale Wy FOS CO13 .....42 A4
Sunnyside Rd RCOLW CO6 .....14 C4
Surrey La K/T/MI CO5 .....62 D4
Sussex Gdns COS CO15 .....60 C3
Sussex Rd COLW CO3 .....25 F5
Sutton Park Av COLW CO3 .....34 A1
Swallow Cl COS CO15 .....59 F3
Swallowdale COLS CO2 .....36 D4
 COS CO15 .....59 F3
Swallow Wk HSTD CO9 .....13 E3
Swan Cl COLN CO4 .....37 F1
Swan Dr COS CO15 .....59 F3
Swan Pas COL CO1 * 2 C5
Swan St K/T/MI CO5 .....52 D3
Sweden Cl HAR CO12 .....10 C3
Sweet Briar Rd COLW CO3 .....23 H5
Swift Av COLN CO4 .....33 H3
Swinbournes Ct RCOLW CO6 * 31 F4
Sycamore Rd COLN CO4 .....27 E4
Sycamore Wy COS CO15 .....64 C1
 FOS CO13 .....41 H5
 MGTR CO11 .....9 E1
Sydney St COLS CO2 .....48 C1
 RCOLE CO7 .....57 E5

T

Tabor Cl RCOLE CO7 .....56 D2
Tabor Rd COLN CO4 .....3 K6
Talbot St HAR CO12 .....11 G3
Talcott Rd COLS CO2 .....36 B5
Talisman Cl K/T/MI CO5 .....63 E2
Tall Trees COLN CO4 .....25 H1
Tamarisk Wy COLN CO4 .....27 F4
Tamworth Cha COLS CO2 .....36 B5
Tangerine Cl COLN CO4 .....37 E1
Tanner Cl RCOLE CO7 .....64 B1
Tapsworth Cl RCOS CO16 .....58 D4
Tapwoods COLW CO3 .....24 D5
Tara Cl COLN CO4 .....27 E3
Tarragona Ms COLS CO2 .....36 C3
Tarragon Cl K/T/MI CO5 .....62 D5
Tawell Ms K/T/MI CO5 .....63 E3
Taylor Ct COL CO1 .....2 C5
Taylor Dr MGTR CO11 .....9 F5
Taylor's Rd K/T/MI CO5 .....49 C2
Teal Cl RCOLE CO7 .....27 H4
Teal Wy K/T/MI CO5 .....52 D4
Tedder Cl COLS CO2 * 36 B3
Telford Rd COS CO15 .....59 H1
Telford Wy COLN CO4 .....19 E5
Temple Cl FOS CO13 .....42 C5
Temple Ct COLN CO4 .....27 E2
Temple Pattle MGTR CO11 .....8 A2
Temple Rd COLS CO2 .....34 D5
Templewood Rd COLN CO4 .....27 F3
Terling Cl COLS CO2 .....48 B1
Tern Cl K/T/MI CO5 .....52 D5
Terndale COS CO15 .....59 F3
Tern Ms RCOLE CO7 .....50 A2
Terrace Hall Cha RCOLW CO6 * 17 F3
The Terrace RCOLE CO7 * 20 D2
Tew Gr K/T/MI CO5 .....63 E2
Tewkesbury Pde COS CO15 * 59 E1
Tewkesbury Rd COS CO15 .....59 E5
Thatchers Dr RCOLE CO7 .....39 E1
Thaxted Wk COLS CO2 .....48 B2
Third Av COS CO15 .....55 E2
 FOS CO13 .....55 E2
 HAR CO12 .....11 F4

HSTD CO9 .....13 G3
Thirtle Cl COLN CO4 .....58 D3
Thistledown COLN CO4 .....26 C1
Thomas Rd COS CO15 .....4 B1
Thomas St RCOLE CO7 .....57 E4
Thomas Wakley Cl COLN CO4 .....18 A4
Thompson Av COLW CO3 .....34 C1
Thomson Av COS CO15 .....59 F5
Thorndon Ct RCOS CO16 .....58 A5
Thorne Rd K/T/MI CO5 .....52 B4
Thornhill Cl FOS CO13 .....42 B4
Thorns Wy WOTN CO14 .....42 C4
Thornton Dr COLN CO4 .....26 A2
Thornwood COLN CO4 .....26 A2
Thornwood Cl K/T/MI CO5 .....67 E4
Thoroughgood Rd COS CO15 .....5 G3
Thorpe Rd COS CO15 .....59 F2
 FOS CO13 .....40 D4
Thracian Cl COLS CO2 .....34 D4
Threadneedle St RCOLE CO7 .....6 C2
Three Crowns Rd COLN CO4 .....25 H2
Three Gates Cl HSTD CO9 .....13 F4
Threshers End COLW CO3 .....34 A2
Thrushdale COS CO15 .....59 F5
Thurlston Cl COLN CO4 .....27 E3
Thurstable Wy K/T/MI CO5 .....63 H5
Tiberius Cl COLN CO4 .....18 C4
Tidings Hl HSTD CO9 .....12 D4
Tiffin Dr K/T/MI CO5 .....63 F3
Tildesley FOS CO13 .....41 E5
Tile House Rd RCOLW CO6 .....17 E1
Tilsit Pl RCOLE CO7 * 20 C2
Timber Hl COL CO1 .....36 D1
Tippett Cl COLN CO4 .....27 E3
Tiptree Hall La K/T/MI CO5 .....62 C5
Titania Cl COLN CO4 .....27 C5
Titus Wy COLN CO4 .....18 C3
Tobruk Rd COLS CO2 .....35 G4
Toga Cl COLS CO2 .....48 A1
Tollgate Dr COLW CO3 .....33 G1
Tollgate East COLW CO3 .....33 H1
Tollgate Rd COLN CO4 .....33 H2
Tollgate West COLW CO3 .....33 H2
Tolliday Cl RCOLE CO7 .....50 A2
Tony Webb Cl COLN CO4 .....18 C5
Tortosa Cl COLS CO2 * 36 C3
Totlands Dr COS CO15 .....59 F2
Totteridge Cl RCOS CO16 .....58 D4
Tournai Cl COS CO15 .....59 F3
Tower Cut RCOLE CO7 .....57 E4
Tower Rd COS CO15 .....4 D6
 RCOLE CO7 .....38 A5
Tower St RCOLE CO7 .....57 E5
Townsend Rd K/T/MI CO5 .....62 D2
Towse Cl RCOLW CO6 .....58 C4
Trafalgar Rd COLW CO3 .....34 B1
 RCOLE CO7 .....20 A4
Trafalgar Yd HAR CO12 * 10 C4
Trajan Cl COLN CO4 .....18 C3
Tree Cl COS CO15 .....59 F2
Trews Gdns K/T/MI CO5 .....52 C3
Trimley Cl RCOS CO16 .....58 B5
Trinity Cl K/T/MI CO5 .....66 D3
 RCOLE CO7 .....50 B2
Trinity Ms HSTD CO9 .....12 C3
 K/T/MI CO5 .....66 D3
Trinity Rd HSTD CO9 .....12 C3
Trinity Sq COLS CO2 * 2 C6
Trinity St COL CO1 * 2 C6
 HSTD CO9 .....12 C3
Trinity Ter HSTD CO9 .....12 C3
Trunette Rd COS CO15 .....64 C1
Tudor Cl COS CO15 .....64 A3
 RCOLE CO7 .....56 D2
 WOTN CO14 .....43 E5
Tudor Ct K/T/MI CO5 * 66 D3
Tudor Rose Cl COLW CO3 .....23 H5
Tudwick Rd K/T/MI CO5 .....63 F5
Tufnell Wy COLN CO4 .....25 F2
Tulip Wk COLN CO4 .....27 E5
Tulip Wy RCOS CO16 .....58 B5
Tumulus Wy COLS CO2 .....34 C5
Turkey Cock La COLW CO3 .....32 D1
 RCOLW CO6 .....23 E4
Turner Av MGTR CO11 .....8 C4
Turner Cl RCOLE CO7 .....50 B1
Turner Rd COLN CO4 .....18 A5
 COLN CO4 .....25 H2
Turnpike Cl RCOLE CO7 .....19 F1
Turnstone End COLN CO4 .....27 G4
Turpins Av COS CO15 .....60 A4
Turpins Cl COS CO15 .....60 A4
Turpins La K/T/MI CO5 .....43 A4
Tusset Ms COLW CO3 .....41 E4
Tweed Cl HSTD CO9 .....12 C4
Twining Rd COLN CO4 .....34 B3
Tydeman Cl HSTD CO9 .....33 H3
Tyehurst Crs COLN CO4 .....26 D2
Tye La COLW CO3 .....38 D4
Tye Rd RCOLE CO7 .....28 D5
Tyler Av RCOS CO16 .....64 B1
Tyler St HAR CO12 .....10 C2
Tylneys Rd HSTD CO9 .....13 F1
Tyndale Dr COS CO15 .....64 A3
Tynedale Sq COLN CO4 .....18 C5
The Tythings HSTD CO9 .....12 C4

U

Una Rd HAR CO12 .....10 B3
Union Rd COS CO15 .....64 A4
Unity Cl COLS CO2 .....36 C3
Upland Crs K/T/MI CO5 .....66 D3
Upland Dr COLN CO4 .....26 D2
Upland Rd K/T/MI CO5 .....66 D3
Uplands Ct COS CO15 .....4 A6
Uplands Rd COS CO15 .....4 A6
Upper Branston Rd COS CO15 .....4 A1
Upper Chapel St HSTD CO9 .....12 D2
Upper Fenn Rd HSTD CO9 .....13 F2
Upper Fourth Av FOS CO13 .....55 F1
Upper Park Rd COS CO15 .....4 B3

RCOLE CO7 .....56 D3
Upper Second Av FOS CO13 .....55 E1
Upper Third Av FOS CO13 .....55 E1
Upper Trinity Rd HSTD CO9 .....12 D5
Upton Cl RCOLW CO6 .....16 A5

V

Vale Cl COLN CO4 .....27 F2
Valenta Cl COL CO1 .....36 D1
Valentines Dr COLN CO4 .....3 J2
Valfreda Wy RCOLE CO7 .....50 A1
Valleybridge Rd COS CO15 .....59 G4
Valley Cl COLW CO3 .....34 B4
Valley Crs RCOLW CO6 .....24 B1
Valley Rd COS CO15 .....59 G4
 COLN CO4 .....10 A5
 RCOLE CO7 .....50 B2
Valley Vw RCOLW CO6 .....24 B1
Valley View Cl COLN CO4 .....18 B5
Van Dyck Rd COLW CO3 .....34 C2
Vanessa Dr RCOLE CO7 .....50 A1
Vansittart St HAR CO12 .....11 G2
Vega Cl COLN CO4 .....18 C3
Ventnor Dr COS CO15 .....59 G1
Ventura Dr COL CO1 .....36 D1
Vermont Cl COS CO15 .....59 C5
Veronica Wk COLN CO4 .....27 E5
Vicarage Gdns COS CO15 .....4 B5
Vicarage La WOTN CO14 .....42 C4
Vicarage Meadow HSTD CO9 .....12 D3
Viceroy Cl COLS CO2 .....36 C4
Victoria Av FOS CO13 .....41 H3
Victoria Cha COL CO1 .....2 A5
Victoria Cl RCOLE CO7 .....38 A5
Victoria Crs MGTR CO11 * 9 E5
Victoria Esp K/T/MI CO5 .....67 E5
Victoria Gdns COLN CO4 .....26 C1
Victoria Pl COL CO1 .....57 E4
 RCOLE CO7 .....57 E4
Victoria Rd COLW CO3 .....35 F2
 COS CO15 .....4 B6
 WOTN CO14 .....43 E3
Victoria St HAR CO12 .....11 G3
Victor Rd COL CO1 .....36 C1
Victor Vls MGTR CO11 * 8 B1
Victory Rd COS CO15 .....4 B2
 K/T/MI CO5 .....66 B4
Viking Wy COS CO15 .....60 D5
Village Cl FOS CO15 .....41 H4
Village Wy FOS CO15 .....41 H4
Villa Rd COS CO15 .....33 H2
Vince Cl K/T/MI CO5 .....66 D4
Vine Dr RCOLE CO7 .....38 B4
Vine Farm Rd RCOLE CO7 .....38 B4
Vine Rd K/T/MI CO5 .....62 C2
The Vineway HAR CO12 .....10 D3
Vineyard Ga COL CO1 .....2 C6
Vineyard St COL CO1 .....2 D7
Vint Crs COLW CO3 .....35 F1
Virginia Cl COS CO15 .....64 A3
Viscount Dr COLN CO4 .....18 D4
Vista Av FOS CO15 .....41 H2
Vista Rd COS CO15 .....5 F1
Vitilus Cl COLN CO4 .....18 C3
Vivian Ct WOTN CO14 .....43 E3

W

Waddesdon Rd HAR CO12 .....11 G3
Wade Reach WOTN CO14 .....42 C3
Wade Rd COS CO15 .....59 H1
Wadley Cl K/T/MI CO5 .....63 F3
Wagtail Pl K/T/MI CO5 * 52 C4
Waldegraves La K/T/MI CO5 .....67 H3
Walden Wy FOS CO15 .....42 C5
The Walk RCOLW CO6 .....23 F4
Wallis Ct COLW CO3 .....34 B4
The Walls MGTR CO11 .....9 F5
Walnut Tree Wy COLS CO2 .....35 H4
 COS CO15 .....62 D1
Walnut Wy COS CO15 .....64 C1
 RCOLE CO7 .....56 D3
Walsingham Rd COLS CO2 .....2 C7
Walter Radcliffe Wy
 RCOLE CO7 .....50 B3
Walters Yd COLS CO2 * 2 C5
Waltham Wy FOS CO13 .....55 G1
Walton Rd COS CO15 .....5 F2
 FOS CO13 .....42 A3
 FOS CO13 .....42 A3
Warde Cha WOTN CO14 .....42 D3
Wargrave Rd COS CO15 .....4 A1
Warham Rd HAR CO12 .....10 B5
Warley Wy FOS CO13 .....55 G1
Warnham Cl RCOS CO16 .....58 B3
Warren La COLN CO4 .....45 G1
Warren Lingley Wy
 K/T/MI CO5 .....63 F3
Warren Rd K/T/MI CO5 .....12 C3
The Warrens FOS CO13 .....42 A5
Warwick Bailey Cl COLN CO4 .....18 A5
Warwick Ct COLS CO2 * 36 D3
Warwick Crs COS CO15 .....4 C1
Warwick Rd COS CO15 .....4 C1
Washford Gdns COS CO15 .....4 B5
Washington Rd HAR CO12 .....10 D5
Wash La COS CO15 .....4 B7
Waterhouse La RCOLE CO7 .....21 H4
Water La COLN CO4 .....25 F4
Watermill Rd K/T/MI CO5 .....53 E2
Waterside RCOLE CO7 .....56 D5
Waterville Ms COLS CO2 .....36 C4
Waterworks Dr RCOS CO16 .....58 B4
Watson Rd COS CO15 .....5 E5
Watts Rd COLS CO2 .....2 C5
Wat Tyler Wk COL CO1 .....2 C5
Wavell Av COLS CO2 .....35 F3

Wavring Av FOS CO13 .....42 A4
Weavers Cl COLW CO3 .....34 C2
Weavers Gn RCOLW CO6 .....14 C3
Weavers Rw HSTD CO9 .....13 E5
Wedgewood Dr COLN CO4 .....25 H2
Weggs Willow COLN CO4 .....3 K5
Weir La COLS CO2 .....48 C3
 K/T/MI CO5 .....49 F2
Wellesley Rd COLW CO3 .....35 H1
 COS CO15 .....4 C6
Well Fld HSTD CO9 .....13 E4
Wellfield Wy FOS CO13 .....41 H4
Wellington Rd HAR CO12 .....11 H1
Wellington St COLS CO2 .....2 B7
 RCOLE CO7 .....57 E4
Well Side RCOLW CO6 .....31 F4
Wells Rd COL CO1 .....3 F4
Well St RCOLE CO7 .....57 E5
Welshwood Park Rd
 COLN CO4 .....27 F2
Wesley Av COLN CO4 .....3 K4
West Av COS CO15 .....4 C5
Westbury Cl RCOLE CO7 .....32 C2
Westbury Rd FOS CO13 .....54 A1
Westcott Cl RCOS CO16 .....58 D5
West Dock Rd HAR CO12 .....10 B2
West Side RCOLW CO6 .....35 F1
West End Rd K/T/MI CO5 .....62 A5
Western Prom RCOLE CO7 .....56 C5
Western Rd RCOLE CO7 .....56 C5
Western's End MGTR CO11 .....9 E1
Westlake Crs RCOLE CO7 .....37 H5
West Lodge Rd COLW CO3 .....35 G1
Westminster Ct COS CO15 * 56 D3
Weston Rd COL CO1 .....3 F4
West Quay RCOLE CO7 .....50 A3
Westridge Rd COS CO15 .....59 E5
West Rd HSTD CO9 .....12 D3
West Stockwell St COL CO1 .....2 C6
West St COLS CO2 .....2 D7
 HAR CO12 .....11 H2
 K/T/MI CO5 .....66 D5
 RCOLE CO7 .....50 A2
 WOTN CO14 .....43 E5
West Vw RCOLE CO7 * 6 C1
West View Cl COLN CO4 .....26 C1
Westway COL CO1 .....2 C2
Westwood Dr K/T/MI CO5 .....67 F4
West Wood Hl COLN CO4 .....25 F2
West Yd HSTD CO9 .....12 C4
Wethersfield Rd COLS CO2 .....48 B2
Wetzlar Cl COLS CO2 * 36 C3
Wetzlar Ct COLS CO2 .....36 C5
Weymouth Cl COS CO15 .....60 D5
W Francis Vls MGTR CO11 * 8 C2
Whaley Rd COLN CO4 .....3 J6
Wheatfield Rd COLW CO3 .....34 A1
Wheatlands RCOLE CO7 .....39 E1
Wheeler Cl COLN CO4 .....37 F1
Whitefriars Wy COLW CO3 .....34 D2
Whitegate Rd RCOLE CO7 .....57 F4
Whitehall Cl COLS CO2 .....48 A2
Whitehall Rd COLS CO2 .....36 D4
White Hart La HAR CO12 .....11 G1
 RCOLW CO6 .....16 B4
White Horse Av HSTD CO9 .....12 C4
Whitehouse La RCOLW CO6 .....24 A1
White Lodge Crs RCOS CO16 .....40 A2
Whitewell Rd COL CO1 .....2 C7
Whittaker Wy K/T/MI CO5 .....66 C5
Wickham Rd COLS CO2 .....35 C2
Wick La RCOLE CO7 .....20 A1
Wick Rd COLS CO2 .....37 E5
Widgeon Pl K/T/MI CO5 .....52 C4
Wilbye Cl COS CO15 .....35 E3
Wilkin Cl COLW CO3 .....34 D3
Wilkin Dr K/T/MI CO5 .....63 E2
Willett Rd COLS CO2 .....35 E4
William Boys Cl COLN CO4 .....27 E3
William Dr COS CO15 .....4 A4
William Groom Av HAR CO12 .....10 D5
William Sparrow Ct
 RCOLE CO7 .....38 B5
William's Wk COL CO1 .....2 C5
Willingham Wy COLN CO4 .....27 F5
Willoughby Av K/T/MI CO5 .....67 E4
Willow Av K/T/MI CO5 .....41 H5
Willow Cl RCOLE CO7 .....56 C4
 FOS CO13 .....41 H5
Willow Pk RCOLW CO6 .....32 D2
The Willows COLS CO2 .....36 B4
Willow Wk K/T/MI CO5 .....62 D1
Willow Wy COS CO15 .....60 A5
 HAR CO12 .....10 C5
 HSTD CO9 .....12 D5
Wilmington Rd COLN CO4 .....26 D2
Wilson Cl RCOLE CO7 .....37 H5
Wilson Marriage Rd
 COLN CO4 .....3 J1
Wilson's La RCOLW CO6 .....31 F4
Wimbourne Gdns FOS CO13 .....42 B4
Wimpole Rd COL CO1 .....36 C1
Winchelsea Pl RCOLE CO7 .....57 E1
Winchester Rd COL CO1 .....36 B2
 FOS CO13 .....55 G1
Windermere Rd COS CO15 .....60 A5
Windmill Cl COLN CO4 * 17 H5
 RCOLW CO6 .....32 D5
Windmill Pk COS CO15 .....59 F4
Windmill Rd COS CO15 .....59 F5
Windmill Vw K/T/MI CO5 .....53 E2
Windsor Av COS CO15 .....4 A3
Windsor Cl COLS CO2 .....36 B5
Windsor Ct RCOLE CO7 .....57 E4
Windsor Rd COS CO15 .....4 A4
 COLS CO2 * 67 E3
Winnock Rd COL CO1 .....36 B1
Winsley Rd COL CO1 .....36 B1
Winsley Sq COL CO1 .....36 C2
Winston Av COLW CO3 .....35 E3
 K/T/MI CO5 .....63 F3
Winston Wy HSTD CO9 .....13 F1
Winstree Rd COLW CO3 .....34 A2

Winstreet Cl COLS CO2 .....34 A2
Winterbournes WOTN CO14 .
Wistaria Pl RCOS CO16
Witch Elm HAR CO12
Witting Cl RCOS CO16
Witton Wood Rd FOS CO13
Wivenhoe Rd RCOLE CO7
Wivenhoe Cross RCOLE CO7
Wivenhoe Rd RCOLE CO7
 RCOLE CO7
Woburn Av FOS CO13
Wolton Rd COLS CO2
Woodberry Wy WOTN CO14
Woodbridge Gv RCOS CO16
Woodcock Cl COLN CO4
Woodcutters COS CO15 .....57 E4
Woodfield Dr K/T/MI CO5 .....31 F4
Wood Field End COLS CO2
Woodford Cl COS CO15
Woodland Cha COLW CO3
Woodland Dr COLW CO3
Woodlands COLN CO4
 COS CO15
The Woodlands RCOLE CO7
Woodland Wy RCOLE CO7
Wood La COLW CO3
Woodpecker Cl COLN CO4
Woodrow La RCOS CO16
Woodrow Wy COLN CO4
Woodrush End COLW CO3
Woodside WOTN CO14
Woodside Av COLS CO2
Woodstock K/T/MI CO5
Woodview Cl COLN CO4
Woolner Rd RCOS CO16
Woolwich Rd RCOS CO16
Worcester Crs RCOLE CO7
Worcester Rd COL CO1
Wordsworth Rd COLW CO3
Worlds End La K/T/MI CO5
Worsdell Wy COLN CO4
Worthing Ms COL CO1
Worthington Wy COLW CO3
Wren Cl COLW CO3
Wrendale COS CO15
Writtle Cl RCOS CO16
Wroxham Cl COLN CO4
Wryneck Cl COLN CO4
Wycliffe Gv COL CO1
Wyncolls Rd COLN CO4
Wyndam Cl COLS CO2
Wyndham Crs COS CO15

Y

Yale Ms COLN CO4
Yarmouth Cl RCOS CO16 *
Yew Tree Cl COLN CO4
Yorick Av K/T/MI CO5
Yorick Rd K/T/MI CO5
York Pl COL CO1 *
York Rd COS CO15
 RCOLE CO7
York St MGTR CO11
Young Cl RCOS CO16
Ypres Rd COLS CO2

76   Acknowledgements

The Post Office is a registered trademark of Post Office Ltd. in the UK and other countries.

Schools address data provided by Education Direct.

Petrol station information supplied by Johnsons

One-way street data provided by © Tele Atlas N.V. Tele Atlas

Garden centre information provided by

Garden Centre Association   Britains best garden centres

Wyevale Garden Centres

The statement on the front cover of this atlas is sourced, selected and quoted
from a reader comment and feedback form received in 2004